YAS

10-6-95

Your *Legal* *Rights*

Also by Elaine Landau

Big Brother Is Watching
Sexual Harassment

*Y*our
L^{egal} *R*^{ights}

*From Custody Battles to School
Searches, the Headline-Making
Cases that Affect Your Life*

Elaine Landau

*Walker and Company
New York*

Copyright © 1995 by Elaine Landau

All rights reserved. No part of this book may be reproduced or transmitted in any form or by any means, electronic or mechanical, including photocopying, recording, or by any information storage and retrieval system, without permission in writing from the Publisher.

First published in the United States of America in 1995 by Walker Publishing Company, Inc.

Published simultaneously in Canada by Thomas Allen & Son Canada, Limited, Markham, Ontario

Library of Congress Cataloging-in-Publication Data
Landau, Elaine.
Your legal rights : from custody battles to school searches, the headline-making cases that affect your life / Elaine Landau.
p. cm.
Summary: Provides a historical overview of children's evolving legal rights and details contemporary cases of child abuse, adoption law, severing ties with biological parents, and more.
Includes bibliographical references and index.
ISBN 0-8027-8359-7. — ISBN 0-8027-8360-0
1. Children—Legal status, laws, etc.—United States—Juvenile literature.   2. Children's rights—United States—Juvenile literature. [1. Law.] I. Title.
KF479.Z9L36   1995
346.7301′35—dc20
[347.306135]   94-42718
CIP
AC

Printed in the United States of America

2   4   6   8   10   9   7   4   3   1

Contents

Your *Legal* *Rights*

1
In Whose Best Interest?

*J*essica DeBoer, a charming two-year-old with large brown eyes and a wonderful smile, had spent her entire young life in a suburban Michigan Cape Cod–style house, where she had her own yellow wallpapered room filled with toys. She'd enjoyed countless good times in her family's backyard playing with their dog, Miles, and she loved watching Barney, the friendly dinosaur, on TV. Since birth her happy, almost idyllic existence had been ensured by the loving, capable couple raising her, Jan and Roberta DeBoer.

The DeBoers were unable to have their own biological children. On their honeymoon, Roberta DeBoer had contracted an infection that eventually led to a hysterectomy. After the DeBoers tried unsuccessfully to adopt for two years, a friend told them about a single woman in Iowa who was pregnant with a child she didn't intend to keep. When Jessica was born her birth mother gave her to the DeBoers, who began the process of adopting the infant. Having the little girl in their lives was a dream come true for the couple.

Jessica's birth mother was twenty-eight-year-old Cara Clausen. At the time of her pregnancy she was employed in an Iowa factory and had just broken up with the baby's birth father, Daniel Schmidt. When Jessica was born on February 8, 1991, Clausen was dating Scott Seefeldt; she put his name on her daughter's birth certificate as the child's father.

At first it seemed as if Clausen was satisfied with her decision to place the baby with the DeBoers. She wrote a letter to the couple saying, "I know you will treasure her and surround her with love, support her, encourage her to dream and to reach for the stars. . . . God bless."[1] The DeBoers secured parental-rights releases from both Cara Clausen and Scott Seefeldt, who they believed was Jessica's father. At that point the DeBoers became the infant's legal guardians, with Jessica's adoption slated to be finalized in six months.

But things didn't go as planned. Shortly after signing the relinquishment papers, Clausen began to have mixed feelings about giving up her daughter. After returning to work she saw Daniel Schmidt, her former boyfriend and the baby's biological father, and told him the truth about what happened. Clausen and Schmidt decided that they wanted their child as well as each other. On March 6, 1991, Cara Clausen filed a motion to retrieve custody of Jessica, while Dan Schmidt did the same shortly thereafter. Within the following months genetic testing irrefutably proved that Schmidt was Jessica's natural father. Since he had never signed away his parental rights, an Iowa court nullified the DeBoers' efforts to adopt Jessica and ordered that the baby be turned over to her birth parents.

But the DeBoers fought back. Initially they hesitated to give up Jessica after learning that the child would have to spend some time in foster care before her birth mother's parental rights could be legally restored. They argued that they and the toddler should not be penalized as a result of what they perceived as Cara Clausen's irresponsible and seemingly erratic behavior.

Although Schmidt married Clausen during this period, some who knew him felt he was hardly an ideal father. Barbara Schlicht, a prior girlfriend of Schmidt's who'd had a daughter, Amanda, with him, found Schmidt sorely lacking as a father. There was also talk that Schmidt had not done enough for still another child he'd fathered with another woman.

While trying to hold on to Jessica, the DeBoers appealed the case to the Iowa Supreme Court. Various child-development experts submitted briefs arguing that removing young

Jessica from her home with the DeBoers could be detrimental to her overall well-being. Professor Albert Jay Solnit, a senior research scientist at the Yale Child Study Center, stated that giving the girl to a couple who might be loving but were nevertheless strangers to her could result in "a loss of intellectual capacity." He stressed that "the hour-to-hour, day-to-day experiences of the first two to three years of life lay the groundwork for the child's personality. One of the basic capacities that children develop in that period is the ability to trust an adult so that they can look ahead to a world that seems to them safe and reasonable, rather than a world that is unpredictable and unstable. These are issues the court cannot afford to ignore." Solnit continued, "The courts shouldn't make the child pay the price of their lawmaking."[2]

Despite such moving testimony the state Supreme Court upheld the lower court's decision. The judge acknowledged that Daniel Schmidt's parenting qualities were questionable and stated that although, for the child's sake, the court was tempted to leave things as they were, legally the natural father's rights had priority over the rights of the child.

In a last-ditch effort to keep Jessica, the DeBoers brought their case before a court in their home state of Michigan, where they finally won their first legal victory. There Justice William Ager of the Michigan Circuit Court ruled that Jessica should remain with the DeBoers since she might never recover from the experience of being taken permanently from the only parents she'd ever known. The judge acknowledged the pain this might entail for the Schmidts, but stressed that "prolonging this battle is going to have a terrible effect on this child."[3] Rejecting the judge's suggestion that they be heroes and allow Jessica to remain with the DeBoers, the Schmidts challenged the Michigan court's authority in the case. Before long, the baby's birth parents could once again rejoice: the Michigan Supreme Court ruled that Michigan had no right to interfere with Iowa court decisions. Jessica had to be returned to the Schmidts in one month.

The DeBoers never actually had a chance of keeping Jessica once the case reached the Iowa court system. Like many other states, Iowa had passed parental-rights laws allowing the biological parents to retain custodial rights forever unless they abandoned the child. Only then would the child's best interests be factored into the custody equation.

Allowing the rights of a (possibly) less than exemplary parent to take precedence over those of a child is abhorrent to many. "We let our government make irrational decisions for children to suffer and be condemned," noted Roberta DeBoer. She and her husband petitioned the U.S. Supreme Court to block the child's transfer, but it refused. She commented: "They're going to walk away just like Michigan did and say, 'We wish we could have done something but there's nothing to do because our laws dictate otherwise.' I wonder if they could take their little two-year-old kids and walk into a black forest and just leave the child and walk away."[4]

The case of baby Jessica set off a loud public outcry. Adoptive parents everywhere wondered if their children could ever count on safely remaining home; their right to do so wasn't recognized under the law. Perhaps these fears were best summed up by Susan Freivalds, executive director of Adoptive Families of America: "Apparently, adult property rights to a child supersede what's best for the child."[5] Her anger was echoed by Sally Stinson, president of the Michigan Association for Infant Mental Health: "You can't just say good-bye to somebody with the idea that you will never see them again and not anticipate that it will be a very difficult lifelong trauma."[6]

Having the legal system view Jessica more as a piece of property than a person did not make leaving the only parents she'd ever known any easier for either the child or the DeBoers. Jan and Roberta tried to put their personal pain aside to make their last weeks with Jessica as pleasant and normal as possible. They continued to take her to the park, sing songs together, and read her her favorite bedtime stories.

When the DeBoers began telling Jessica that she'd be

leaving them, the child would say, "No, I'm not going," and begin to cry. Although everything was done to comfort her, on the day she left, the toddler was carried from her home screaming "Mommy . . . I want my dad. Where's my dad?" There had been no way to legally stop the parental switch. "I thought someone very high up would say, 'I just can't watch this,'" commented a friend of the DeBoers, but it never happened.[7]

Jerome Smith, professor at the School of Social Work at Indiana University, summed up Jessica's plight: "She really will not be able to understand what's going on. She will see tears rolling down their cheeks. No matter what assurances they try to give her, it will not fill the bill."[8] Yet in the end the two-and-a-half-year-old seemed to have some idea of what had happened. "The court gave me away," she said sadly.[9]

Nearly a year after Jessica went to live with the Schmidts, they began giving television and newspaper interviews to show the world how well Jessica, whom they had renamed Anna Jacqueline, had survived the ordeal. However, some child-development experts were skeptical that any child would adjust quickly and easily in such a difficult situation. Sally Rutzky, one of the guardians appointed to oversee Anna's best interests during the Michigan hearings, had remarked, "You really don't know what will happen with a crack in the foundation until it's asked to weather some external force."[10]

The rights and best interests of children have frequently been overlooked in similar court dramas. One such unsettling incident occurred in Connecticut in 1991 when a teenager entered a New Haven hospital under an assumed name and gave birth to a baby girl. Hours later she fled the facility, leaving her infant behind. The authorities searched for her and for the baby's biological father; when they were unable to locate either parent, the infant was put up for adoption.

Over the next few months the baby thrived in a secure home with loving parents who were anxious to adopt her. But then the birth mother reappeared, claiming that she wanted her daughter back. If she won custody, the baby would be taken from a stable environment and sent to live with her natural mother in a shelter for homeless people. Nevertheless, in 1992 the Connecticut State Supreme Court ruled in the teenager's favor. The legal decision evoked an angry public outcry from those concerned about the infant's welfare and future. "The best interests of the child were totally ignored," noted the state health commissioner. "What was worshiped was the technicality of the law and the mystique of blood ties."[11] This has proven true in many situations.

2
A Shameful History Continues

*T*he history of children's rights is bleak internationally. Not only were rights for young people virtually unheard of during much of the past but the further back we look in history, the poorer the level of childcare and the more doubtful a young person's survival to adulthood.

In antiquity, baby-killing (or infanticide) was fairly common. Writings from ancient Greece are replete with children tossed into rivers or left on hills and roadsides, where they either died from exposure to the elements or served as prey for birds and wild beasts. Illegitimate children, both boys and girls, were regularly killed up until the nineteenth century. Even children born to married couples might be killed, if they had a slight deformity or were sickly or cried too much.

If the firstborn child was a healthy male, he was usually allowed to live. Girls were considerably less valued and therefore more readily doomed. The population records retrieved from one town in ancient Greece, for example, reveal that there were 118 sons in the locale as compared with twenty-eight daughters. Generally, males far outnumbered females until the Middle Ages when the practice of infanticide slowed down.

Of course, child abuse still occurs. But many common child-rearing practices of early times would now be completely unacceptable. Swaddling, or tightly wrapping infants in lengths of cloth, was thought necessary to keep babies from scratching out their eyes, tearing at their skin, or breaking their bones. Swaddling was a cumbersome procedure: It could take up to two hours to securely wrap a child. But parents readily did so because a swaddled infant was significantly easier to care for. And because people believed that newborns should remain asleep, a swaddled baby might be placed behind a warm oven, hung from a peg on the wall, or generally "left like a parcel in every convenient corner."[1] Children were sometimes so tightly bound that their circulation was cut off and gangrene set in.

The absence of children's rights in past centuries is exemplified by the consistently poor treatment of youths. Whippings were an acceptable aspect of disciplining young people and even a year-old baby might feel the "rod" if his parents thought it necessary. The famous composer Beethoven hit his students with a knitting needle, and on some occasions even bit them! Not even royalty was spared. For example Louis XIII of France was beaten as a child.

In describing how she punished her four-month-old infant, one mother wrote: "I whipped him till he was actually black and blue, and until I could not whip him any more and he never gave up one single inch."[2] Today a parent who treated a child that way might be arrested, but in past centuries children were routinely brutalized by their mothers, fathers, and teachers.

Youths in colonial America fared somewhat better, safeguarded to a degree by the nature of the economy. In the New World all family members toiled together for their mutual survival. During this period most families produced nearly all of what they needed. Men and boys cleared and plowed the land, then planted, cultivated, and harvested what was grown. When they weren't farming they performed necessary repairs on their houses, barns, and fences, fed and cared for the livestock, and kept the farm equipment in working order.

Females were comparably busy with other important

tasks. Women and girls did the cooking and cleaning and made all the family's clothing, soap, and candles from scratch. They cultivated small kitchen gardens and were responsible for childcare.

Children were put to work as soon as they were old enough to earn their keep. Young children quickly learned what they needed to know to grow up and be productive members of society. Nearly everyone worked from dawn to dusk and was exhausted by the day's end. That left little opportunity for parents to become embroiled in disputes with their children. So, ironically, colonial parents' fatigue, lack of recreational time, and need for farm help often combined to act as a protective shield of sorts for their offspring.

This did not mean that colonial children were treated as their parents' equals. The father was the indisputable head of the household. His wife came second in the hierarchy, although women had no legal standing and were not permitted to enter into contracts. Children had even less status; they were expected to be hardworking and obedient at all times.

The New England colonists were so concerned with correcting impropriety in young people that in 1641 they enacted legislation known as the Body of Liberties to ensure that minors knew their place. According to these laws any youth over sixteen who either cursed or struck his parent could be put to death. In 1645 the Massachusetts General Court extended the use of the death penalty to cover stubborn or rebellious young people as well:

> If a man have a stubborn or rebellious son, of sufficient years and understanding (viz.) sixteen years of age, which will not obey the voice of his Father, or the voice of his Mother, and that when they have chastened him will not harken unto them: then shall his Father and Mother being his natural parents, lay hold on him, and bring him to the Magistrates assembled in Court and testify unto them, that their son is stubborn and rebellious and will not obey their voice and chastiment, but lives in sundry notorious crimes, such a son shall be put to death.[3]

This provision placed severe restrictions on a youth's behavior. Yet since the displeased parents had to bring the accused child before a court, he or she was afforded some protection under the law, at least the right to a hearing prior to being condemned under a law that is unjust and brutal by today's standards. While such safeguards might seem minimal, this was the first legislation anywhere in the world to afford any legal protection to minors. However, the rights accorded youths by the Body of Liberties were never put to the test. No supposedly "stubborn" or "rebellious" child was ever saved by the law since no angry parent ever actually took a case to court.

An assessment of the rights of colonial young people is further complicated by the fact that many children did not grow up at home with their families. Depending on the sex and number of offspring a couple had, some might be sent out to live with other families. Frequently such young people were taken in by relatives or neighbors who needed additional workers. These youths enhanced the economic status of their keepers while relieving their parents of the burden of feeding them when there were already sufficient family members to work the land. Girls residing with other families did housework, while boys labored in the fields. Both were frequently treated more like overworked servants than like extended-family members. These mistreated young people had no legal recourse and were expected to do as they were told. If they failed to meet the expectations of the families or businesses for whom they worked, they might be brutally punished.

Orphans often found themselves in this position after being auctioned off by the authorities to families or businesses needing cheap labor. Conditions were especially difficult on the tobacco plantations in the Chesapeake region of Maryland, where the work was exhausting and malaria was rampant.

Orphanages were created as havens for youths who had been worked nearly to death or who had endured excessive

corporal punishment at work. But these orphanges failed to
be the sanctuaries for parentless children some hoped they'd
be. Large numbers of young people were overworked, given
little nourishment, and severely whipped at these institutions. The following is a description of a boy who ran away
from a Georgia orphanage and was brought to court on June
6, 1741, to demonstrate what conditions were typically like
at such facilities:

> It was yet too visible from scars and wounds not yet healed,
> that great cruelty had been used; It was not denied that the
> boy was made naked to the waist, after the manner of com-
> mon malefactors, and lashed with five strong twigs tied to-
> gether, as long as they would hold, whereby his whole back,
> shoulders, loins, flank, and belly were in a dreadful condi-
> tion.[4]

In severe cases such as the one described above, the state
had the power to remove the child. However, these children
were often sent to work for a family or company under comparably bad conditions. In the mid-1700s people viewed
child abuse very differently than they do today. Young people
were supposed to be grateful for the opportunity to earn
their keep.

Most colonial American children worked either at home
or on farms. But when the Industrial Revolution began in the
1740s and created a need for cheap labor, children were
among the nation's first factory workers. Child labor had
been essential to the growth of industry in England, and
America took its cue from the British. This was a sad turn of
events for young people on both sides of the Atlantic. British
children five years of age and older were made to work two
consecutive sixteen-hour shifts in dark, dank factories without decent food or fresh air.

At these English facilities, several children would share
the same worn mattress. When someone got up to go to
work, another child would sink down for a few hours of sleep
before returning to his or her place at the machines. As one

onlooker described the children's predicament, "In stench, in heated rooms, amid the whirling of a thousand wheels, little fingers and little feet were kept in ceaseless action, forced into unnatural activity by blows from the heavy hands and feet of a merciless onlooker."[5]

Among the worst work environments in the United States were Pennsylvania's coal mines.

> The boys sat for ten or eleven hours a day in rows on wooden boards placed over chutes through which tons of coal constantly passed. Their task was to pick out from the passing coal the slate, stone, and other waste that came from the mine. The slate so closely resembled the coal that it could be detected only by close scrutiny. The boys had to bend over the chute and reach down into it. Even if they wore gloves, which was not always possible because they had to rely on a sense of touch, the moving material was so sharp that it could cut and tear their hands. The position in which the boys sat was not only tiring but backbreaking, causing obvious round shoulders and narrow chests. If a boy reached too far and slipped into the coal that flowed beneath him, he stood little chance of surviving intact.[6]

Despite its inhumanity, child labor continued to be eagerly sought by American manufacturers. Young people worked for nearly nothing, and businessmen believed them to be "more tractable, reliable and industrious, quicker, neater and more careful" than adults.[7] In fact, some employers only hired adults on the condition that their children come to work as well.

In an effort to rectify the terrible conditions under which children toiled, the National Child Labor Committee was formed in 1904. Largely functioning as a children's advocacy group, the organization worked to push through legislation to dramatically curb child labor. Insisting that childhood was sacred and that young people had a right to feel safe and secure during their formative years, the organization issued the following statement:

"It should be plainly said that whatever happens in the sacrifice of adult workers, the public conscience inexorably demands that children under twelve years of age shall not be touched; that childhood shall be sacred; that industrialism and commercialism shall not be allowed beyond this point to degrade humanity. Thus the function of the Committee will be a preventative one. By no other means than those suggested can the needless sacrifice of child life be prevented."[8]

The committee gathered information on the worst child-labor cases and began to publicize the problem and push for reformist legislation. Its efforts led to tough child-labor laws in a number of states. The organization also campaigned for the creation of a national child-labor bureau, which was established in April 1912. The mission of the Children's Labor Bureau was to look into "all matters pertaining to the welfare of children and child life among all classes of people, and . . . [to] investigate the questions of infant mortality, the birth rate, orphanages, juvenile courts, desertion, dangerous occupations, accidents, and diseases of children, employment [and] legislation affecting children" throughout the United States.[9]

As time passed, public support for child-labor reform grew. This was partly due to the continuing educational campaigns launched by the National Child Labor Committee and to the creation of the U.S. Children's Labor Bureau. But what made the horror of child labor real for many Americans was a tragic fire in 1911 at the Triangle Shirtwaist Company in New York City. The fire consumed the top three floors of the factory and took the lives of over 140 workers, many of whom were children. There was only one fire escape, and workers had to climb through a small window to reach it.

"Boys and girls crowded out on the many window ledges and threw themselves into the streets far below. They jumped with their clothing ablaze. The hair of some of the girls streamed up aflame as they leaped. Thud after thud sounded on the pavement. It is a ghastly fact that on both the Greene Street and Washington Place sides of the building there grew mounds of dead and dying. And the worst horror of it all was that in this heap of the dead now and then there stirred a limb or sounded a moan."[10]

Yet even after the fire, reformers did not succeed in sustaining national legislation to ban brutal child-labor practices. The two bills passed by Congress to protect children were later declared unconstitutional by the U.S. Supreme Court, which saw the laws as interfering with states' rights to handle "local" matters. Children's-rights activists also failed to have a constitutional amendment passed curtailing child labor. Supporters of the movement refused to give up, however, and in 1938 Congress finally passed the Fair Labor Standards Act, which contained a provision regulating child labor. The act banned the employment of children under sixteen years of age in industries involved in interstate commerce (which is where the federal government has jurisdiction). It further barred people less than eighteen years old from working in hazardous occupations such as manufacturing, mining, and logging. While the Fair Labor Standards Act was challenged the same way previous antichild labor legislation had been, it was nevertheless upheld by the U.S. Supreme Court.

The Fair Labor Standards Act provided the clout needed by reformers who wanted to recapture childhood for children. Yet despite significant advances, some degree of illegal and offensive child labor still exists in America today. It is perhaps most obvious among migrant farmworkers.

While other children play with dolls or video games, migrant farmworkers and their families travel from state to state to pick crops. The harvests are seasonal. Farmworkers on the East Coast may pick oranges in Florida, head for Georgia for peaches, and go to South Carolina for the harvest of tomatoes and cucumbers. Then it's north to New York to harvest peas, cabbage, and cherries before returning to Florida to pick oranges again. Generally, these families move six or seven times a year. The child workers rarely attend any one school for more than three months at a time. Those enrolled frequently miss days or weeks to help their parents in the fields. When they do go to school they are often ridiculed because of their shabby clothes and where they live. In any case, few migrant child laborers go past the ninth grade, and many unofficially stop attending school long before that.

The working and living conditions endured by these children are frequently deplorable. At times families camp on the beach or in a park while on a job. Many have no choice but to rent the substandard shelters offered by the growers who hire them. These shelters range from leaky tents to mildewed shacks with cardboard walls. Some employers convert broken-down school buses or vans into housing for the pickers. The dwellings are usually furnished only with cots or mattresses. Several family members may share a mattress, and if there isn't enough space for everyone, some of the children sleep on the floor with only a blanket. Often there is no electricity, running water, or indoor toilet. No medical benefits are provided on these jobs, and tuberculosis, viral infections, and malnutrition run rampant in migrant camps where poor sanitation is the norm. Most children's teeth rot, because they rarely if ever see a dentist.

The young people are expected to work from daybreak to sundown during the harvest, adhering to the same schedule as adult laborers. The growers provide them with stale and nearly inedible food, for which their families are charged exorbitant prices. In some cases, working conditions can be especially hazardous. Hundreds of thousands of migrant workers are sickened every year by the pesticides used on the crops. When sharp cutting utensils are needed for the work, there are frequently serious accidents as well. The growers and crew leaders who hire and supervise the migrant families operate their farms and orchards in blatant violation of the Fair Labor Standards Act and other laws designed to protect workers of all ages.

"It's a disaster," says Marvin Feingold, an attorney for the Neighborhood Legal Assistance Program based in

Charleston, North Carolina. "The farmer is only interested in getting the crops in and the crew leader is a law unto himself. Meanwhile the migrant worker is being exploited."[11] Similar feelings are voiced by Roger Rosenthal, executive director of the Washington-based Migrant Legal Action Program, "The working conditions and treatment of migrant workers . . . are horrendous—a throwback to the early unregulated days of American agriculture. . . . The U.S. Department of Labor has not committed the human and financial resources that are needed to enforce the laws."[12]

While all workers suffer from the lack of government inspectors assigned to migrant camps and the light fines levied on growers for infractions of the law, the children are most affected. They are still dependent on their parents and there is little they can do to improve their predicament. Living on the fringe of American society, often such children are invisible. They remain continually on the move, missing Census Bureau counts as well as services available through the Department of Health and Human Services. Despite the efforts of reformers, these young people are still habitually exploited and deprived of what they need to reach their full human potential. Regardless of how many laws have been passed, their reality hasn't changed very much over the years.

3
The Right to Protection from Abuse and Neglect: One Step Forward, Two Steps Back

*T*he scene was a quiet New York City courtroom in 1874. A small girl named Mary Ellen McCormick stepped up to the witness stand and changed the way in which society and the legal system viewed children's rights. Her story underscored every child's basic entitlement to a life free from physical and emotional abuse.

> My name is Mary Ellen McCormick. I don't how old I am.
> . . . I have never had but one pair of shoes, but can't recollect when that was. I have not had shoes or stockings this winter. . . . I have never had on a particle of flannel. My bed at night is only a piece of carpet, stretched on the floor beneath a window. . . . Mamma has been in the habit of whipping and beating me almost every day. She used to whip me with a twisted whip, a raw hide. The whip always left black and blue marks on my body. I have over on my head two black and blue marks which were made by Mamma with the whip, and a cut on the left side of my forehead which was made by a pair of scissors in Mamma's hand. She struck me with the scissors and cut me. . . . Whenever Mamma went out I was locked up in the bedroom. . . . I have no recollection of ever being in the street in my life.[1]

How did this happen to Mary Ellen? Her mother, Frances Conner, came to New York from England in 1858 and worked as a hotel laundress. She met and married an Irishman named Thomas Wilson. Soon afterward, Wilson was drafted into the army; Frances Conner gave birth to a baby girl, Mary Ellen.

Within the year Wilson was killed in battle, and the young mother was forced to find work to support herself and the infant. She couldn't afford a baby-sitter while she worked so she used her entire army widow's pension as partial payment to a woman to take in her child. The infant's new home was a small airless apartment in an overcrowded tenement. Mary Ellen's "foster mother" took the baby only for the money; three weeks after Frances Conner proved unable to pay her full fee, she turned the little girl over to the city's Department of Charities.

Mary Ellen was placed in an orphanage and later taken in by Thomas and Mary McCormick. The state did not investigate the couple; the McCormicks were merely required to report from time to time on the girl's condition. Mary Ellen wasn't with them long before Thomas McCormick died. His widow married a man named Francis Connolly. For the next six years Mary Ellen was repeatedly beaten, made to work long hours, and locked in a closet for days at a time; she was rarely bathed, or even spoken to kindly. Although annual reports about the girl were to be filed with the Department of Charities and Correction, only two reports were ever sent in.

Finally, in late 1873, young Mary Ellen's plight came to the attention of Etta Wheeler, a social worker in the area. She'd been contacted by Connolly's landlady who'd noticed that the child had been abused. The Connollys moved, but the social worker eventually found them.

It was December and the weather bitterly cold. She [Mary Ellen] was a tiny mite, the size of five years, though, as afterward appeared, she was then nine. From a pan set on a low stool she stood washing dishes, struggling with a frying pan about as heavy as herself. Across the table lay a brutal whip of twisted leather strands and the child's meager arms and legs bore many marks of its use. But the saddest part of her story was written on her face in its look of apprehension and misery, the face of a child unloved, of a child that had only seen the fearsome side of life.[2]

Although Etta Wheeler had seen many cases of child neglect and abuse, the severity of Mary Ellen's case was particularly distressing to her. She asked the police to intervene but was told they needed concrete evidence of an assault before they could act. The charitable institutions Wheeler approached agreed to care for the child temporarily but noted that she could be placed with them only through legal means. That left the social worker facing a perplexing problem: There *were* no legal avenues by which a child could be forcibly removed from an abusive home.

Yet Wheeler came up with a creative solution to the problem. Since the child was technically a member of the animal kingdom, she contacted Henry Bergh, founder of the American Society for the Prevention of Cruelty to Animals, to intervene on Mary Ellen's behalf. Bergh's lawyers went before Judge Abraham R. Lawrence and described the girl's predicament, arguing that since the Connollys had never legally adopted Mary Ellen they had no right to keep her. The attorneys also offered a list of witnesses willing to testify that Mary Ellen was in danger of being maimed or killed. Bergh himself testified that his actions were not connected to his animal-rescue work as he didn't want to equate children with animals. But he hoped the legal system would act to prevent the needless cruelty inflicted on young people.

Judge Lawrence cleverly invoked a little-known law to create a new method to remove children from dangerously abusive homes. A warrant was issued under Section 65 of the Habeas Corpus Act, which provided that if someone was illegally being confined—kept prisoner—and his or her life or safety was jeopardized, the authorities could bring the person to court so as to resolve the issue legally.[3]

As a result of this action Mary Ellen was taken from her home and brought into court. Since she didn't have sufficient clothing of her own, the police officers fetching her had to wrap her in a blanket. A reporter present described the situation: "I saw a child brought in . . . at the sight of which men wept aloud, and I heard the story little Mary Ellen told . . . that stirred the soul of a city and roused the conscience of a world . . . and as I looked, I knew I was where the first chapter of children's rights was being written."[4]

Mary Connolly, the woman Mary Ellen called her mother, was subsequently charged with assault and battery, assault with intent to do bodily harm, assault with intent to maim, and assault with intent to kill. Not only Mary Ellen but also several neighbors and the social worker Etta Wheeler testified against her. Mary Connolly was indicted for assaulting the young girl with a pair of scissors and for the continual battering endured by Mary Ellen during 1873 and 1874. The jury deliberated for only twenty minutes before finding the woman guilty. She was sentenced to a year of hard labor in the city penitentiary. Her guilt and punishment were significant in setting a legal precedent for future child-abuse cases.

Mary Ellen never returned to the Connolly home, but since no living relations could be found she was handed over to the Department of Charities and Corrections. This division handled juvenile cases and grouped minors together in the same institutions regardless of whether they were delinquents or merely orphaned. So ten-year-old Mary Ellen was placed in a reformatory with teenaged girls who'd committed criminal acts.

Seeing that Mary Ellen was about to become the victim of still another injustice, Etta Wheeler persuaded the judge to turn the child over to her. Mary Ellen was raised by Wheeler's sister in a country environment in upstate New York. "They taught her to play, to be unafraid, to know her rights and to claim them. She shared her happy, busy life from the making of mud pies to charming birthday parties and was fast becoming a normal child."[5]

Mary Ellen matured, married, and had children of her own. She was a loving mother; fortunately, the terrible experiences of her own childhood did not negatively affect her own child-rearing practices. "To her children, two bright, dutiful daughters, it has been her joy to give a happy childhood in sharp contrast to her own," said Etta Wheeler.[6] Later on, when presenting a paper entitled "The Finding of Mary Ellen" at a meeting of the American Humane Society, Wheeler said, "If the memory of her earliest years is sad, there is this comfort that the cry of her wrongs awoke the world to the need of organized relief for neglected and abused children."[7]

Mary Ellen's experience led to the founding of the New York Society for the Prevention of Cruelty to Children (SPCC). The society's initial purpose was to intervene legally on behalf of severely neglected and abused minors. In time it expanded its scope to include child abandonment and the exploitation of children for monetary gain. At the urging of the SPCC, New York passed a state law in 1885 prohibiting children under fourteen years old from working. But although many hoped they'd never see another case of child abuse like Mary Ellen's, many children today find themselves in similar situations. Recent reports from the House Select Committee on Children, Youth and Families indicated that child abuse, especially neglect and sexual abuse, is on the rise.

A case in point is that of "Johnny," a baby who came to the authorities' attention because his mother neglected him. Johnny had a cold and fever that developed into pneumonia. After he was hospitalized, it was obvious to the medical staff that the small boy had not been properly nourished and cared for.

Johnny was placed in foster care for a time before being returned to his mother. Yet his home still left much to be desired. Johnny lived in a single room, in a squalid welfare hotel. Besides coping with the facility's poor maintenance and services, residents also had to contend with considerable violence both in the building and in the surrounding neighborhood. Johnny's situation was especially troublesome because his mother, who was mentally retarded, had never acquired adequate parenting skills.

As Johnny was already showing signs of delayed development, he was referred to an early-intervention program. Specialists there were supposed to help the boy and also assist his mother in improving her parenting. But it proved extremely difficult for Johnny's mother to comprehend what she needed to do to adequately meet her son's basic needs. Having to bring up the child in an overcrowded potentially dangerous home environment only added to the severity of the situation.

Over the next two years Johnny came to the early-intervention program daily. Sometimes he'd need a bath or be so tired that he'd just fall asleep. He was often inappropriately dressed and failed to bring snacks that were fit to eat. Even though he enjoyed coming to the program, Johnny was often temperamental and unruly. While only two years old, he often became so violent that the staff found him difficult to control.

With the passage of time the young boy's condition deteriorated. Often, he didn't come to the center. At other times he did arrive but looked unkempt and wore filthy clothes. Johnny had frequent temper tantrums and grew even harder to handle. Yet perhaps most disturbing to the center staff were the unexplained marks and bruises they sometimes noticed on his body. When they reported the boy's condition to Child Protective Services he was once again taken from his mother.

Initially Johnny did not adjust well to foster care. The first family he was placed with couldn't handle his emotional outbursts and sometimes violent behavior. Days later he was moved to a second placement with a family willing and able to tackle Johnny's special needs. Living with them, the small boy finally began to thrive.

During this period Johnny's social worker arranged visits with his mother as well as with his three brothers, who were also in foster care. After the mother's boyfriend was charged with the physical and sexual abuse of her children, she promised to sever her relationship with him. And the family was found a new apartment in a safer neighborhood.

About a year later the court returned Johnny to his mother's care. He continued coming to the center, and before long the staff noticed new bruises and fresh cigarette burns on him. After Child Protective Services was called, Johnny was again removed from his home. Although the signs of physical abuse healed quickly enough, Johnny was emotionally traumatized by his early life. By the time he was five years old, he was an angry, violent youngster who had difficulty controlling his impulses and conforming to normal behavioral expectations. Years of treatment might be needed to turn his life around—if that was even possible.

Child abuse is readily condemned by society. Federal, state, and local laws have been passed prohibiting this injustice, yet children throughout the country are still mistreated every day of their lives. The problem stems partly from the fact that the rights of the individual are regarded as sacred in the United States, and the legal system has long been concerned with safeguarding parental rights. Too often the courts fail to consider that children are individuals as well; as a result, children's rights frequently come second to those of adults.

The following is typical of what usually occurs in cases of child abuse or severe neglect: Someone, perhaps a neighbor, teacher, relative, or family friend, reports the abuse to Child Protective Services or a comparable government agency by dialing a toll-free number. The agency investigates the complaint, and intervenes if the allegations are true. Usually intervention involves removing the child or children from the home and placing them in foster care.

Once a child is taken from his or her home, the court system is brought into the case. Evidence of the abuse is presented to justify the young person's removal from his or her home. In most instances the court orders the social-service agency involved to make certain that the parent is given every opportunity to have his or her offspring returned. Depending on the case, this may mean ensuring that the parent receives counseling, money, and help finding a better place to live.

Throughout this period the young person remains in foster care. He or she not only has to cope with the effects of abuse or neglect but also must adjust to a new environment and to the foster parents and their expectations. This can be extremely stressful for the child, who may receive counseling.

But despite such efforts to help, children who enter foster care often have emotional and behavioral problems. These signs may be evident in abused children as young as two. They may have long temper tantrums, secretly hide food, and be aggressive toward other children. Even when therapists work with foster families to help children see that stability and consistency can be part of their lives, the children are often slow to respond and trust. And who can blame them?

When the child and his or her biological parent are both believed to be on an even keel, the social service agency may arrange for them to visit each other. Ideally, by then the parent has learned all he or she needs to know to properly care for the child, and has worked through whatever psychological or substance-abuse problems were standing in the way of good parenting. While some parents are able to improve thanks to the services offered them, many are not.

Often the only genuine change that occurs is that a social worker finds the family a safer and perhaps more comfortable place to live. Sometimes a child's home improves if the parent has gotten a job or if the government has supplied financial help. But while these cushions are important, they are not a substitute for behavioral changes on the parent's part. No parent can be rehabilitated unless he or she is willing to make the necessary changes. If the parent merely accepts the material advantages social services provides, but doesn't behave any differently, the child still suffers. Often he or she becomes a victim, without rights, resources, or recourse.

"Kevin," a baby boy born to an unwed teenaged mother, is a prime example of how things can go wrong. Kevin first came to the attention of the Department of Social Services in Washington, D.C., when he was just ten days old: His mother had abandoned him in the emergency room of St. Elizabeth's Hospital. The two were eventually reunited. During his early years at home Kevin's mother hit him, wouldn't let him play with other children, and made him sit on the toilet for long periods in a futile effort to toilet-train him. Once the small boy even attempted suicide by continually banging his head against the wall with as much force as he could muster.

When he was three, Kevin was taken from his mother—but he was returned to her when the court order that enforced the separation lapsed because of a careless mistake. Less than a month after that, Kevin was again brought to St. Elizabeth's emergency room. He was obviously neglected, and the staff also suspected abuse. While at the hospital Kevin climbed into a garbage can, and when a nurse asked him what he was doing, he told her that he was worthless and ought to be thrown out with the rest of the trash.

Through the years Kevin endured at least a dozen "social-service placements"—many foster homes, and a group facility. He also had at least eight different social workers, which only added to the instability of his life. His return trips to his mother, compounded by the other negative aspects of his existence, took their toll. Kevin was eventually institutionalized because he had severe psychiatric and behavioral problems.[8]

Another, perhaps even more distressing incident involved Joseph Wallance, a three-year-old Chicago boy who'd spent the majority of his short life in foster care. The boy's mother, Amanda, was emotionally unstable and had been in and out of mental institutions for years. Nevertheless, she pleaded with the court to allow her to regain custody of her son. "I want to give him love, affection, something I didn't have,"[9] she argued. The judge agreed to return Joseph to her, but the decision came at the preschooler's expense. Barely two months later Amanda was charged with murder: Her small son had been hanged with an electrical cord.

There is no limit on the number of times a child may be returned to a home in which he or she has been neglected or abused. And, unfortunately, every year thousands of children are returned to such homes. There is no legal safety net to rescue them.

Part of the problem is the difficulty of legally terminating parental rights. In the United States, people charged with crimes don't have to prove that they're innocent. Rather, a person is presumed to be innocent until proven guilty. Therefore, a parent accused of abuse does not have to prove to the court that he or she is capable of constructive parenting. Instead, the state has to convince a judge that the parent in question is unfit. Even when children have been temporarily removed from a dangerous home, the parent does not have to do much to show that he or she has changed.

"Our system is not designed with specific guidelines that force abusive parents to show strong evidence of remediation or show that they are capable of caring for a child," explain child-development experts Karen Dorros and Patricia Dorsey. "It is not uncommon for a parent to contact the child [just] once in six months, but on the basis of that visit alone, the natural parent's rights would not be terminated. Visiting your child [for] an hour once in six months seems to be a very poor standard of commitment, particularly for a parent who already has abused a child."[10]

Because of laws that ensure parental rights and the autonomy of the family, there is little a social-service agency can do to protect the rights of children in these situations. Social workers are often forced to continue working with parents who fail to make genuine plans to better care for their offspring and may still be secretly abusing drugs and alcohol. Some parents even deliberately undermine the child's placement to make themselves look better. While visiting the child, they make unflattering remarks about the foster family or falsely promise that when the child comes home things will be different and they'll all be off to Disneyland.

Even when the child is finally returned and little has actually changed, it may still take time for the social worker to build a case strong enough to terminate the parent's rights. Judges readily react to tangible abuse such as beating, burning, and starvation. They're often hesitant to respond to the scarring effects of severe emotional abuse and to less concrete forms of violence and neglect. Thus social workers often have to wait until the home situation becomes nearly catastrophic. Sometimes a child's needs and rights are only considered after he or she has nearly been killed.

Because the government agencies that are supposed to safeguard children actually enforce laws slowly—if at all—many children's-rights activists feel that the agencies are nearly as much to blame for abuse as parents are. The seriousness of the situation prompted the American Civil Liberties Union (ACLU) to establish the Children's Rights Project in 1979. This group affords abused and neglected minors a strong voice in a system in which they're often overlooked.

In many cases the rights of these young people are violated even more frequently than those of most children since many of them are poor and members of minority groups. The ACLU wanted to ensure that when the state intervenes in a child's life, it does so without violating the rights and privileges guaranteed to that young person by the U.S. Constitution. The Children's Rights Project's attorneys hoped to make certain that child-welfare systems in America provide necessary services impartially and without discrimination.

Besides the problem of child-welfare agencies and courts repeatedly returning young people to abusive homes, the ACLU Project cited the following injustices that frequently befall abused and neglected minors:

Thousands of children placed in foster care programs are shuttled from one home to another, causing their education and emotional development to be disrupted.

Children are often placed in homes with untrained and poorly supported foster parents, under the supervision of poorly trained and enormously overworked social workers.

Children who are eligible for adoption must wait for years for an adoptive family, or are never adopted at all, often simply because administrators have failed to do the paperwork.[11]

The organization further described the plight of children caught up in a mismanaged foster-care system.

They are irreparably damaged. They are denied the prerequisite for healthy development: a stable home. They suffer the emotional trauma of growing up in circumstances of perennial uncertainty, not knowing whether or where they will be moved, who will care for them, when or if they will ever have permanent homes. Their emotional problems are aggravated, or they develop new psychological and behavioral problems—including depression, hyperactivity, and learning disabilities—in direct response to the disruptions of foster care. In short, they are deprived of the opportunity for a normal childhood.[12]

These wasted childhoods are costly not only to the young victims but also to society at large. The Children's Rights Project states that of the children who left the foster-care system in 1991, 25 percent were homeless for at least one night, 40 percent went on public assistance or welfare, 46 percent dropped out of school, and over half were eventually among the unemployed. Many of these children are likely to remain at least partly dependent on state subsidies throughout their lives. Yet if they'd received the help they needed when they were children, this might not be the case.

The Children's Rights Project tried to rectify the situation through litigation as well as through the threat of taking social-service agencies to court to force them to improve their performance. In initially assessing the work ahead, project attorneys knew that theirs would not be an easy task. Funding for child-welfare agencies, which was crucial to their effective functioning, could be cut at any time by whoever happened to hold state or federal office. To make the situation worse, recordkeeping was not always up to par, and that made it exceedingly difficult to track children precisely. Nevertheless, lawsuits had previously been used successfully to reform prisons, schools, and facilities for the mentally ill and retarded; Children's Rights Project lawyers set out to do the same for child-welfare systems throughout the country. The Children's Rights Project's pioneering lawsuits were based on the Constitution: "[an] individual's right to due process and equal protection under the law, and their right not to be harmed while under the control of the state."[13]

The efforts of the Children's Rights Project are sorely needed since the number of young people in the foster-care system has steadily climbed in the 1980s and 1990s. While the majority of minors remain in foster care an average of 1.4 years, the Children's Rights Project also found these disturbing statistics: 10 percent spend at least 7.4 years in foster care; 14 percent spend at least five years without a permanent family; and a quarter stay in foster care for 4.3 years or more.[14]

Many of the project's legal challenges resulted in landmark cases that strengthened and expanded the rights of children caught up in the system. An example of these advances was the project's 1989 suit on behalf of Kevin (the young boy who climbed into a trash container because he felt worthless) and all the other children affected by Washington, D.C.'s Department of Human Services. In the suit *LaShawn A. v. Bareny*, project lawyers argued that the District's foster-care system violated the constitutional rights of the children in its care and was "in a state of ongoing crisis as severe as that experienced by many of the homes from which the system is removing children."[15]

To substantiate these charges, project attorneys gathered

extensive evidence revealing that in addition to other short-comings the Department of Human Services had not inves-tigated claims of child abuse and neglect promptly, had inadequately monitored the large number of already overcrowded foster homes in which children were placed, and had too few workers to properly oversee its cases. It was not unusual for a social worker to carry a caseload of ap-proximately 100 young people.

The Children's Rights Project also learned that the D.C. area's child-welfare system had neither found enough adop-tive homes nor provided adequate assistance to the chil-dren's biological parents. As a result, young people in the District of Columbia spent an average of five years in foster care, as compared to the national average of seventeen months. Much of the problem had to do with the depart-ment's money shortage. It would be difficult for any child-welfare system to properly function with a too-small staff and without a broad range of programs and services. The D.C. agency, however, was so disorganized that it even failed to claim the $21 million a year in federal aid it was en-titled to!

The suit against the agency went to court in February 1991. At the end of the three-week trial the Children's Rights Project and the foster-care children of the District were vic-torious. The court described the area's foster-care system as a "travesty" and ruled that the agency had violated the young people's constitutional rights as well as a number of laws in-tended to ensure their welfare. "Although these children have committed no wrong," the judge noted, "they in effect have been punished as though they had."[16] This was the first time an American foster-care system was found to be operating in violation of the law.

In response, the District of Columbia's child-welfare sys-tem embarked on a plan to restructure itself. The Depart-ment of Human Services doubled its staff of licensed social workers and required that its workers be better trained. Fos-ter-care payments were also raised to enable the agency to recruit more qualified families, and interaction between foster parents and agency personnel was improved as well. In addition, record-keeping procedures were revised so children could better be tracked.

The Children's Rights Project achieved a similar victory in Connecticut. In 1989 the project and the Connecticut Civil Liberties Union sued the state's child-welfare system. The problems in Connecticut were much like those of the District of Columbia: The child-welfare system was woefully understaffed; reports of abuse and neglect sometimes went unchecked; and foster families were insufficiently trained and poorly compensated.

In the summer of 1991 an out-of-court settlement was reached. The state of Connecticut agreed to enhance its child-welfare system while both the Children's Rights Project and the Connecticut Civil Liberties Union monitored the system's overhaul to ensure that the changes were accomplished.

In addition to the important results achieved in the District of Columbia and Connecticut through the project's work, other vital measures have been implemented elsewhere. Kentucky took steps that would speed a young person's adoption or return to his or her natural parents, so as to shorten time spent in foster care. Training for both social workers and foster parents in Missouri was strengthened, and social workers' case loads were limited. The Children's Rights Project has clearly demonstrated that providing a powerful voice for children within the legal system is essential to ensure children's rights.

When child-protective agencies fail at their job the results can be devastating. That's what happened to "Adam," who lived in New York City with his four brothers and one sister, his mother, his father, and his grandfather. Family problems were first noticed by a hospital staff member who called a child-abuse hotline to report that two of Adam's brothers were being beaten by their mother "unnecessarily and excessively." It was also believed at the time that Adam's mother had been sexually abused by his father. In seven years, from 1983 to 1990, at least a dozen incidents of child abuse and neglect involving Adam's family were reported.

Although the New York City Child Welfare Administration was aware of the problem, none of the incidents was ever thoroughly investigated. Meanwhile, over the years hospital and police files continued to thicken with descriptions of the physical and sexual abuse endured by the five children in the small boy's family. There was documentation on broken limbs, a fractured skull, a crushed finger, and a wide range of bruises over large areas of the children's bodies.

Yet instead of intervening, the Child Welfare Administration allowed the children to remain in their hazardous home. In fact in 1988, just three days before Christmas, for some unknown reason the child-protective agency even closed the case. A little over two months later, New York City's 47th Police Precinct was called to investigate the death of a five-year-old. The medical examiner determined the cause of death to be "multiple blunt impact injuries to the head, chest, abdomen, and extremities with laceration of the liver and hemoperitoneum [internal bleeding] due to fatal child abuse."[17] The dead child was Adam.

A comparably horrific case that made headlines in newspapers throughout the country was that of six-year-old Lisa Steinberg. Perhaps Lisa captured the nation's attention because, coming from an upper-middle-class household, she defied the stereotype of the neglected and abused child without rights. Lisa's biological mother was a young unmarried Catholic woman, Michelle Launders; she gave up the newborn for adoption to afford her the best possible start in life. Joel Steinberg was the young woman's adoption lawyer. He agreed to her request that the baby be placed with a Catholic family and even told her that he had just such a couple in mind. Steinberg described the prospective adoptive father as a well-off attorney and the mother as a contented homemaker. Launders was anxious to make a good impression on the adoption lawyer so that he would take the case and place her baby in the wonderful environment he described. Although all expenses in a private adoption are generally paid by the couple receiving the child, Michelle and her mother were required to give Steinberg $500 for his services. At no time did they ever imagine that he had no intention of finding a home for the baby; instead, he and his live-in lover, Hedda Nussbaum, would keep the child for themselves.

Launders's daughter, Elizabeth (Lisa) Steinberg, spent her short life in an apartment in a five-story Greenwich Village town house that was once Mark Twain's home. Unfortunately, apartment 3W—the Steinberg-Nussbaum residence—was now a dwelling characterized by pain and violence. Joel Steinberg was a temperamental, brooding man who was often quick to act out his rage. A former girlfriend said, "He had a violent temper and would explode without reason."[18]

Hedda Nussbaum was a bright, attractive children's-book editor who eventually became one of Steinberg's victims. Early on in their relationship, she began coming to work with dark glasses on. They hid her freshly bruised eyes and cheeks. In January 1978 she was so badly beaten around the eye that she sought treatment for the injury at a nearby hospital.

In time, it became increasingly difficult for Nussbaum to placate Steinberg. Some nights he would not permit her to sleep in their bed, instead making her lie on the floor with only a pillow and blanket. When he was angry at her, he would take away the pillow. As the years passed, the violence further escalated. In February 1981 Nussbaum was savagely attacked by Steinberg; the beating was so severe that her spleen had to be removed. Later a metal exercise bar smeared with blood and hair that matched Nussbaum's would be found in the apartment.

It was into this environment that Michelle Launders's infant was brought shortly after her birth on May 14, 1981. In an attempt to block the adoption, some of Nussbaum's friends and co-workers reported Steinberg's violence to the authorities. But, because the lawyer knew that his volatile relationship with Nussbaum could not withstand the scrutiny of a court-ordered review, the couple never even attempted to legally adopt little Lisa. Hedda Nussbaum returned to work after securing the child, frequently keeping the sleeping infant at her side. A colleague remembered that one day the baby had a cut lip, and Nussbaum had come to work wearing a bandage and sunglasses.

Tenants in the building where Steinberg and Nussbaum lived revealed that slaps, curses, and bloodcurdling screams often emanated from the couple's apartment. Sometimes the sound of a falling body could be heard as the seemingly relentless beatings continued through the night. The neighbors felt powerless to do anything. The police were called frequently, but Hedda Nussbaum continually refused to press charges. It was obvious that she was a battered woman, but at the time few thought that young Lisa, whom Steinberg seemed quite taken with, had become his victim as well.

Nevertheless, looking back, the signs of child abuse and neglect were all too evident. In the months before her murder, six-year-old Lisa often seemed unhappy. An older child at school noticed that she'd cry when it was time to go home. Formerly bright and alert, Lisa had grown increasingly listless and depressed. Her appearance also seemed to indicate neglect. She frequently looked unkempt—for example, she came to school with her hair badly matted. When the teacher asked the child how she'd gotten some very noticeable bruises, Lisa lied out of fear and said that her little brother (another child illegally kept by Steinberg and Nussbaum) had hit her. The teacher questioned Steinberg about the bruises as well, but he gave the same well-rehearsed story.

Ironically, Lisa Steinberg was nearly rescued twice during the last month of her life. On October 6, 1987, the police arrived at apartment 3W after being called by a neighbor who'd heard screams. Initially Steinberg tried to keep the officers out, insisting that he was aware of "his rights." However, a sergeant finally maneuvered his way past the angry attorney and demanded to see Nussbaum. After a time she timidly emerged from the couple's bedroom. She had a swollen lip, and it was obvious that she'd been beaten, but as usual she refused to sign a complaint. Unable to take further action, the officer left her a pamphlet explaining her rights and where battered women could go for assistance. Sadly, the rights of the children in the apartment were entirely overlooked.

Only two weeks later Steinberg was driving on the New York State Thruway when an alert toll-taker noticed the small bruised and sobbing girl in the car with him. The toll-taker phoned the police, who stopped the car further down the road. But Steinberg managed to convince the officers that nothing was the matter. He claimed that he was an attorney on his way home with his young daughter after trying a drug-trafficking case in Albany. He added that his daughter was crying because she'd injured her neck. The police were satisfied with Steinberg's explanation. Lisa was sent home.

On November 1, 1987, Steinberg slept late. Because the children were up and hungry, Nussbaum cooked some vegetables for them. When Steinberg arose and began dressing for a business meeting at a restaurant, Lisa asked Nussbaum if she'd be going along. The young girl enjoyed these outings and eagerly looked forward to them. Nussbaum said she didn't know Steinberg's plans and told Lisa to ask him herself. The young girl went into the other room to do so. That was the last time Nussbaum saw the child conscious.

Soon afterward Steinberg approached Nussbaum. He was carrying Lisa in his outstretched arms. When she asked him what had happened he answered, "What's the difference?" But he later explained that Lisa had annoyed him by looking at him too intently. "I knocked her down and she didn't want to get up again," Steinberg said of the unconscious six-year-old. "This staring business has gotten to be too much."[19]

While Nussbaum tried to revive Lisa, Steinberg continued to dress for his appointment. Before exiting the apartment, he instructed Hedda, "Don't worry, just let her sleep. I will get her up when I get back."[20] However, Steinberg did not return for over three hours. Meanwhile Lisa remained unconscious on the floor; water and undigested food oozed from her small mouth.

Nussbaum was no help to the child. She checked Lisa's pulse and tried to pump her chest, but Lisa did not respond. The woman later said in court that she thought everything would be all right because she believed Steinberg had "healing powers." "I looked at the phone and I started thinking, 'Should I call 911 or . . . a pediatrician?' And I said, No, Joel said he would take care of her. . . . And I didn't want to show disloyalty or distrust for him. So I didn't call."[21]

When Steinberg finally returned to the apartment, the couple freebased cocaine; Lisa still lay unconscious. Finally, at 6:33 the following morning, Hedda Nussbaum called the New York City emergency switchboard to say that her daughter had choked on an early-morning snack. Within minutes an ambulance and police car arrived on the scene.

The first officer to enter the apartment was appalled by what he found. None of the lamps or lighting fixtures worked although the electricity hadn't been turned off. The rooms were devoid of decoration. The foul odor of rotting food and filth permeated the apartment. Amid this squalor, Lisa's sixteen-month-old "adopted" brother, Mitchell, sat tied to his playpen by a three-foot rope. The baby wore only a urine-soaked diaper. He didn't have a crib, but slept in the playpen. (Lisa had usually slept on the living room couch.) Steinberg and Nussbaum shared the apartment's only bed, on which bloodstained sheets and pillowcases were visible.

The police officer immediately bent over Lisa, trying to revive her. The child wasn't breathing, but she still had a pulse. He couldn't help but notice that the small girl's naked body was covered with bruises.

Hoping to save Lisa's life, the officer hurriedly carried her from the apartment. The ambulance waiting below took her to St. Vincent's Hospital, where doctors immediately set to work on her. Lisa did not recover. She'd suffered a brain hemorrhage caused by repeated blows to her head. For three days, the six-year-old remained in the hospital, hooked up to a mechanical respirator. During that time the nurses who cared for Lisa lovingly nicknamed her Sleeping Beauty.

Finally, Lisa was declared brain-dead, and the life-support system was disconnected. Joel Steinberg was charged with manslaughter, while Michelle Launders came to claim her daughter's body. She told a judge that she didn't want Lisa buried next to the people responsible for her death. Lisa's baby brother was more fortunate. His biological mother claimed him and took him to live with her.

Lisa Steinberg's right to life and happiness was ignored by the people who cared for her and by the societal systems authorized to protect minors. Unfortunately such insensitivity to the rights and needs of young people has often left children around the globe in dire straits. In some South and Central American nations, young people abandoned by their families may be left to starve and live on city streets; in several African countries boys as young as seven and eight have been carried off by the army to serve as soldiers.

But in 1994 Michael Fay, an American teenager residing with his mother and stepfather in Singapore, brought a particularly distressing incident to the public's attention. Fay, a high school student, was arrested along with several other foreign-born teens after being accused of spray-painting several cars, throwing eggs at vehicles, and switching license plates on some automobiles. Although in October 1993 Fay confessed to engaging in a ten-day vandalism spree with the other young men, he later recanted this confession, insisting that he was subjected to nine days of sleep deprivation and repeated beatings by Singapore police. In a letter smuggled from his prison cell to his father in America, Fay noted that he'd been continually hit by an interrogator who threatened to whip him. "I don't truly know who did it [the crime] and everything that I admitted was a lie."[22]

Several Singapore attorneys said that the teen's allegations of police brutality were likely to be true. In fact a fifteen-year-old Malaysian arrested with Fay for the crime was so severely beaten while in custody that his eardrum was punctured. A recent report from the U.S. State Department also confirmed the use of torture as an interrogation tactic. There had been, said the report, "credible reports of police mistreatment" in Singapore.[23]

Although Fay pleaded guilty to two counts of vandalism and two counts of mischief only after being assured that he wouldn't be caned, on March 3, 1994, a judge sentenced the teenager to six strokes of the cane, four months in jail, and a $2,300 fine. Caning is a form of corporal punishment in which a prison officer trained in martial arts strikes a prisoner on the bare buttocks with a half-inch-thick rattan cane that has been moistened to prevent it from splitting. Each stroke of the cane usually breaks open the person's skin, causing profuse bleeding and leaving permanent scars. The procedure is so painful that victims frequently go into shock before the beating is over.

President Clinton asked Singapore's government for clemency, but although Fay's sentence was reduced to four strokes, the caning was nevertheless carried out, on May 5, 1994. In response the President said: "I think [the caning] was a mistake . . . not only because of the nature of the punishment related to the crime, but because of the questions that were raised about whether the young man was in fact guilty and involuntarily confessed."[24] Fay's caning did not bode well for the prospect of leniency in the case of seventeen-year-old Hong Kong–born Shiu Chi Ho, still another youth arrested and convicted with Fay. In addition to being given a long jail term, the boy was sentenced to twelve strokes of the cane—a punishment some find unusually harsh considering Shiu's age and lack of a criminal record. Human rights organizations and many diplomats believe that caning constitutes a major human rights violation and that the nation's brutality casts a dark cloud over Singapore's international reputation.

While tremendous advances in child protection have sometimes been achieved through diplomatic, legislative, and courtroom efforts, the daily lives of many youths still do not reflect these changes. Until attitudes change and young people are universally accorded the same human and civil rights as adults, child protection may remain in its present state of one step forward, two steps back.

4
Standing Up for Their Rights

Divorce has become commonplace in America. Husbands and wives who no longer wish to be legally bound to one another are free to find new spouses and start new families. But what about children? Should unhappy young people have the right to "divorce" their parents and select new ones?

That was the case with twelve-year-old Gregory Kingsley. Gregory wanted to divorce his mother and have the foster parents he was living with adopt him. By hiring a lawyer and taking the case to court himself, Gregory became the first child in America to sue to sever his ties with a biological parent.

The boy's decision was deeply rooted in his memories of an unstable and unhappy childhood. His mother, Rachel Kingsley, a high school dropout from St. Louis, Missouri, married her husband, Ralph, when she was just seventeen years old. She gave birth to Gregory about a year later and had two other sons, Jeremiah and Zachariah, soon after.

While Rachel was pregnant with her third child, her husband left. The boys remained with their mother, but when Gregory was four and Jeremiah three she permitted them to leave for a month-long visit with their father in his new home in Denver, Colorado. They were supposed to be back by the end of November, but after several months their father still hadn't returned them. Early the following year Rachel decided to retrieve her children herself, but she wasn't able to wrench Gregory from his dad. "I finally decided in March to go and steal them back," said Rachel. "I got Jeremiah but he wouldn't give me Gregory. I didn't see Gregory again for five years."[1]

Rachel later moved to Orlando, Florida, to look for a better job, leaving her two younger sons with her sister to complete the school year where they were. When her sister began having her own marital problems, however, she turned the boys over to the state of Missouri. The state contacted Ralph, who picked up the children and took them, along with Gregory, to Florida. There Ralph tried to reconcile with Rachel, but things didn't work out. Before long he and Gregory moved out of the home they all had together, even though Gregory would have preferred to stay with his mother. When Ralph was later charged with both abusing and neglecting the boy, Rachel finally regained custody of her eldest son.

The children were happy to be reunited, but their joy was shortlived. Their mother now worked as a waitress for $2.15 an hour plus tips and received no child support from her husband. Under these circumstances she often found it hard to meet her expenses. Seeking assistance, she contacted the Florida Department of Health and Rehabilitative Services (HRS), which, she claims, suggested that she put her two older boys in foster care until she was better able to provide for them. "First you lose the phone," Rachel explained. "Then the electric . . . They took my boys—and that was the most awful feeling."[2]

The children remained in foster homes for nearly a year, but Rachel visited them regularly. Once she settled on an apartment and a roommate, the state returned her sons and they finally felt like a family again. But that situation fell apart as well. Rachel's roommate moved out, and when she couldn't afford the rent on her own they lost the apartment. She had promised the children they'd never be separated again, but at that point Rachel Kingsley saw few available alternatives. For a second time, her two oldest sons were placed in foster care. "I had to take Gregory down to HRS with his little suitcase," she recalled. "He handled it like a little man, but he didn't want to leave me."[3]

The state placed Gregory at a residence hall known as Lake County Boys' Ranch. At about the same time, a newly formed commission was established to study local services for children. Among its members was a local attorney named George Russ. While visiting the facility, Russ happened to notice a young boy reading a book. The child, who'd looked up at Russ as he passed the room, stirred something within the attorney. "I probably saw him for thirty seconds. For some reason something struck me about the child," he recalled. "I have to tell you, I have eight children of my own. I was not looking for another child. I am a rational person. I am not impulsive. But I couldn't get him off my mind."[4]

Russ began making inquiries about the boy and a few weeks later, he and his wife, Lizabeth, visited Gregory at the residence hall. They liked him immediately and were moved by the fact that more than anything Gregory wanted a secure home of his own. The Russes began foster-parent training, and Gregory started visiting them on weekends. But after just two weekends, the twelve-year-old confronted the couple with the possibility of making their relationship permanent. "Am I going to live with you from now on?" he asked. When the Russes asked if Gregory meant living with them as a foster child, the boy replied "No, I mean forever and ever."[5]

In October 1991 Gregory moved in with the Russes as a foster child. He mixed well with their other children and at times the whole family felt as if he'd always been with them. But before long Gregory again began asking the Russes to adopt him. The couple wanted him as their son, but they were afraid of disappointing Gregory in the event that things didn't work out. Yet they were also hopeful that the adoption would proceed smoothly, since Rachel Kingsley hadn't phoned or written Gregory since he'd come to live with them. But shortly thereafter they were faced with the unsettling news that Rachel Kingsley wanted her oldest son back.

When Gregory's mother placed her children in foster

care for a second time she was told she'd have to take a number of steps before bringing them home. These requirements included taking parenting courses, attending counseling sessions, and successfully proving to Florida state authorities that she was emotionally and financially capable of caring for her offspring.

About six months after agreeing to these specifications, Rachel decided to return to Missouri and move in with a male friend. An interstate "parent-performance contract" was drawn up; Rachel had until May 1992 to meet its requirements. Her lawyer later claimed that her client thought she only needed to meet the requirements within the specified time, but in actuality she was expected to periodically file progress reports and keep in closer touch with her sons. When Rachel Kingsley failed to do this, officials assumed that she didn't plan on having her children returned to her. They were ready to sever her parental rights, paving the way for Gregory's adoption.

Ironically, it was Rachel's husband, Ralph, who started the process of trying to have the boys returned to their mother although he had not been in touch with either her or the children. When he learned that they were back in foster care, he requested an emergency hearing before a Florida judge. Rachel and her boyfriend drove down from Missouri to be in court that day. The judge agreed to give the boys back to Rachel, and she was allowed to take Gregory's younger brother Jeremiah home with her.

But now she had a new problem she hadn't counted on: Gregory didn't want to leave his foster placement to return to Missouri with his mother. When Rachel heard that the family he was with wished to adopt Gregory, she refused to consent, believing this would settle the matter. But after an HRS social worker suggested that she get a lawyer, Rachel Kingsley realized there could be some serious roadblocks ahead.

Gregory was extremely angry with his mother for refusing to free him for adoption by the Russes. He didn't want to live with his mother, but his foster father explained that he'd have to do whatever the judge handling his case determined. When Gregory asked how he could make the judge see things his way, Russ explained that Gregory could present his perception of the situation in court. "I told him . . . that in my opinion, he is a citizen of the United States and that there are certain rights that citizens have: equal protection under the law, due process of law; access to court; the right to life, liberty, and the pursuit of happiness," Russ explained. "It follows, then, in my opinion, that he has the right to an attorney of his choosing, and that he has the right to bring a lawsuit in his own name."[6] Gregory was enthusiastic about this approach.

Although Russ said he couldn't act as Gregory's lawyer, he gave him the name of someone who could. Gregory's attorney was Jerry Blair, a woman who'd previously taken on and won some high-profile juvenile cases. Blair admired the twelve-year-old's courage in challenging the system and "fighting back." Describing her young client as "trying to take responsibility for his life," she noted that Gregory did not have a relationship with his mother and believed that if he were sent home, he'd eventually end up back in the foster-care system.

In July 1992 a Florida judge determined that Gregory's case could proceed, underscoring the premise that the boy had the same right as any other American to protect his own interests. While child-custody cases are not uncommon, Gregory's was the first in which the minor in question was actively involved in shaping his own destiny. His suit was slated to be heard in court late that September.

As the court date approached, Rachel Kingsley's arguments for regaining custody of her child seemed to carry less weight, and Ralph had agreed to Gregory's adoption by the Russes and had signed the necessary consent forms. HRS had also recommended that Rachel Kingsley's parental rights be terminated so that the Russes could adopt Gregory.

Rachel's plea for Gregory was further weakened by her

present home situation. Steve, the man she lived with, had a criminal record; the couple's relationship had already been marred by violent outbursts. Just weeks before Gregory's court date Michigan police received an emergency call from his eight-year-old brother, Zachariah. Having dialed 911, the child hysterically reported that his mother "was being pushed down the stairs." When the police arrived, they found Rachel Kingsley bleeding and badly bruised. Zachariah informed the police that Steve was responsible for his mother's injuries.

Besides failing to provide a safe home for herself and her children, Rachel Kingsley had shown herself to be a less-than-ideal parent. Testimony during the two-day hearing revealed that she had frequently left the boys unattended, drank excessively, smoked marijuana in front of the children, and angrily slapped the boys on their heads. Although other testimony was moving, perhaps the most compelling witness was twelve-year-old Gregory. When asked why he wanted to sever his relationship with his biological mother, he answered, "I'm doing it for me so that I can be happy."[7]

The result of the hearing reaffirmed that although Gregory Kingsley was a minor, he had certain inalienable rights guaranteed him by the Constitution. A round of applause resounded through the courtroom when the judge announced "I believe by clear and convincing evidence, almost beyond a reasonable doubt, in this case that this child has been abandoned by statutory definition and neglected by Rachel Kingsley. And Gregory, you're the son of Mr. and Mrs. Russ at this moment."[8] Gregory's attorney presented him with a blue jersey bearing his new name and the number 9, "his" number as the Russes' ninth child. Now living happily with his new family, he's a young man who made history in the realm of children's rights.

The issue of children having a say in who their parents will be was also brought to the forefront in the case of fifteen-year-old Kimberly Mays, who went to court to sever ties with her biological parents, Ernest and Regina Twigg. Her story began in 1979 at Hardee Memorial Hospital in rural Wachula, Florida. Somehow delivery-room identification tags were switched, sending Kimberly and another baby girl home with the wrong parents. No one realized that there'd been an infant exchange until 1988, when the child the Twiggs named Arlena died due to a debilitating heart defect. Genetic testing shortly before the girl's death revealed that Arlena was not the biological child of either Ernest or Regina Twigg.

As Kimberly Mays was the only other white baby girl born in the hospital at that time, the Twiggs were anxious that she be tested to determine if she was their daughter. Robert Mays, Kimberly's father, agreed to have the tests performed if the Twiggs would not seek custody if Kimberly proved to be theirs. According to published reports, on November 20, 1989, testing showed almost certainly that Kimberly Mays was actually a Twigg.

As their arrangement did not preclude Ernest and Regina Twigg from asking for visitation rights, in 1990 Kimberly began regularly seeing her biological family. Some said that Kimberly seemed happy enough in video footage taken with her birth parents and seven brothers and sisters. But after only five visits Mr. Mays cut off any further interaction claiming that it had been too unsettling for Kimberly. Supposedly the time she spent with the Twiggs had taken a toll on both the girl's attitude and school performance.

The Twiggs retaliated by seeking custody of the girl. In 1992 a judge refused to take Kimberly from the home she'd grown up in. Nevertheless, the young teen wanted to be sure she'd always have a say about her future and be able to remain with Robert Mays, the man she'd called her father all her life. She therefore went to court to "divorce" the Twiggs, hoping to permanently sever their connection.

Reportedly the ninth-grader adamantly turned against her birth parents after Mrs. Twigg publicly voiced her unproven suspicions that the babies were deliberately switched at the hospital. Barbara Coker Mays (Robert Mays's first wife, who died when Kimberly was two) was from a prestigious local family that allegedly had some sway at the hospital. It was also believed that Mrs. Twigg's characterization of Robert Mays as an abusive and unfit father further alienated Kimberly. Several times during the court proceedings the young girl repeated, "I want them out of my life. I want my life back."[9]

In his ruling on the case, Judge Stephen Dakan noted that Mrs. Twigg had repeated those unsettling accusations in letters sent to the editor of Kimberly's hometown newspaper, and signed other people's names to the correspondence. "It would be difficult to conclude that this conduct showed substantial concern for the welfare of Kimberly," the judge stated. He added that the Twiggs' stand appeared to be that their interests, whatever they might be, were paramount.[10]

As in the case of Gregory Kingsley, the court determined that Kimberly was entitled to the constitutional guarantees of privacy and the pursuit of happiness regardless of her age. In accordance with the teenager's wishes, he ruled that Robert Mays was her legal as well as psychological father. "To declare [the Twiggs] to be her natural parents," the judge wrote, "requires more than evidence that they be her biological parents."[11] Unlike Baby Jessica's case described in chapter 1, where Iowa law did not permit the court to consider the interests of the child, Florida law afforded the judge more leeway.

Feeling that Kimberly was still too young to decide to exclude them, the Twiggs asked that their visitation rights be restored. But the judge believed it might be damaging for Kimberly to have to see her biological parents against her will, and ruled that the 1989 visitation agreement between the two families was no longer valid.

George Russ, Gregory Kingsley's adoptive father, served as one of Kimberly Mays's attorneys in her suit against the Twiggs. In assessing the outcome, he said: "It was a pure situation of psychology versus biology and the court made it clear where it comes down."[12] Similar sentiments were expressed by Harvard Law School professor Elizabeth Bartholet, who suggested that the ruling represented growing legal recognition of the preferences and emotional needs of minors. "It's time we move beyond the notion that just because you are the birth parents, you automatically have parental rights," said Bartholet. "In terms of psychological and emotional reality, it just doesn't make a lot of sense."[13]

When Kimberly Mays's attorneys first telephoned her with news of the favorable verdict, she was reportedly relieved and quoted as saying that "she wanted to kiss the judge." Yet within a year the story took an ironic turn: The following March, word leaked to the media that Kimberly Mays had run away from home. Initially the girl sought shelter at a YMCA youth haven in Sarasota, Florida, but eventually wound up where most people thought she'd be least likely to go: the Twiggs' home. It was agreed that Kimberly would informally remain with the Twiggs for a time, without any further court battles. Later, an informal shared-custody agreement was worked out. When asked about his client's change of heart, George Russ replied that Kimberly was "just a young girl having some problems common to many teenagers. There's no dirt there, no sordid soap opera."[14]

Kimberly Mays's turnabout was not as significant for children generally as her court victory was. The teen's successful legal challenge inspired both children's-rights advocates and many young people dissatisfied with their family situations and in search of an avenue for change. While sociologists and legal scholars ponder whether young people have the insight and maturity to pick their parents, increasing numbers of young people are beginning to assert themselves in this arena. Instead of running away from home or suffering in silence as past generations had, growing numbers are now attempting to "divorce" their parents.

A case in point is that of twelve-year-old Jillyin Flecker. Although Jillyin loved both her parents, she wasn't happy with her home life. "We moved into a little house which had hardly any furniture; one mattress for all six of us kids to sleep on. My Dad would beat up on my Mom a lot and most of the time in front of the kids. Our house was filthy. I was really young and it was all just too much for me to take."[15] Jillyin further described her father as an alcoholic who was also "addicted to marijuana"; her mother, she said, was an alcoholic too.

After moving to North Carolina Jillyin's mother contacted a local church, which proved quite helpful to the family. Jillyin attended Pioneer Girls meetings there every Wednesday evening and soon became close to Cathy Flecker, the group's leader. Before long Jillyin was spending more and more time with the Flecker family. "Well then . . . [I] would spend nights over there and have dinner with them and you know I found out what a good family they had. And then I— One summer, I went to stay with them because my— my Mom said that she wasn't going to be able to entertain me for the summer. And so Cathy said that she'd take me— that I could go home with her."[16]

After continuing to stay with the Fleckers, Jillyin knew that she wanted to be with them permanently. But sometimes when visiting her biological family the young girl felt that her parents were hesitant to let her return to the other household. Wanting a sense of permanence to her relationship with the people she regarded as her second family, Jillyin resorted to legal measures. She asked her parents to relinquish their parental rights so the Fleckers could adopt her. "Because I can't go back, because after I've lived with the Fleckers, . . . I found . . . that there's a better way to live. That it's not just . . . money or anything," said Jillyin. "It's—I found love. . . . I know that my parents love me and I know they still do. But I guess it was expressed to me [by the Fleckers] in the way . . . I needed it to be."[17]

Jillyin's parents acknowledged their daughter's right to have the home she wanted. They let the adoption proceed. They later regretted their decision, however, and wanted their daughter back. At one point they even accused the

Fleckers of brainwashing the girl, and denied that their home life was as troubled as Jillyin portrayed it. Jillyin's biological mother described her perception of what occurred: "I just believe that they tried to alienate my daughter from us and the things that she said about us, you know, the facts that she's written down, they're not truth. . . . And it's just things that have been told her that, you know, she shouldn't have to put up with that. And—and, you know, she deserved better which I know she, you know, deserves niceness."[18]

The demands of Jillyin's biological family placed the girl in a difficult situation. She especially missed her siblings and did not want to alienate anyone by doing what she believed was best for herself. Yet Jillyin stood by her decision to remain with her adoptive parents, and in doing so served as an example to other youths to assert themselves. In a letter to a talk-show host, she wrote, "I want to be able to tell other children going through similar situations that there is hope and not to give up. They need to realize that even as children we have rights."[19]

Besides pursuing an active role in securing the parents and home life they deserve, young people have begun to stand up for their rights in other ways. Among these pioneers in children's rights is Desiray Bartak, a young sexual-abuse survivor. The trauma that changed Desiray's life began when she was just ten years old. During her summer vacation from school, she was visiting her father (Desiray's parents were divorced). On such visits Desiray usually spent some time at the home of her godfather, Richard Streate, who also had children. One evening after they and Desiray had eaten submarine sandwiches and played Nintendo, she slept over at their house.

But Desiray didn't rest peacefully. During the night Richard Streate crept into her room and molested her. Too frightened to oppose him, the ten-year-old pretended to be asleep. Trying to block out what was happening, she told herself "It's a dream. Don't believe it, it's a dream. It's not happening."[20] Yet the young girl felt as if that "dream" went on forever.

The following day neither Desiray nor her godfather spoke about what had occurred. But Desiray felt a loss of control and knew that her rights as a human being had been violated. "I felt that if your godfather can do this to you, who was supposed to love you and take care of you and you're supposed to trust him, then anyone can do it to you."[21]

The impact of Streate's actions was searing. Upon returning to her mother's home Desiray appeared markedly upset. Her formerly harmonious relationship with her mother and sister soon became characterized by frequent arguments and angry outbursts. Desiray later admitted that she'd hesitated to tell her mother what had taken place. "Even though me and my mom were so close, I didn't think that she would believe me because he was so close to the family, and I was afraid that he would hurt someone in my family if I told."[22]

Desiray sank into an extended depression. Her grades dropped, and she had difficulty sleeping. Even when she was able to rest, Desiray was plagued by hideous nightmares. "I didn't feel that I should live my life anymore because it was over. There was nothing left for me to do," she recalled.[23]

Although she still hadn't told her family what happened, Desiray began therapy to try to work through her pain. But when she went to visit her father the following summer, she was expected to spend time in the home of the man who'd molested her. Desiray described her reaction to seeing Streate again as follows: "He opened the door and I saw that look on his face. I felt like ten million pounds of bricks just hit me and fell right on my shoulders. And I was crying for my Dad not to leave, 'cause I didn't want him to leave, but I didn't tell him why. And that night he [Streate] approached me and tried to again."[24]

This time Desiray kept the covers tucked tightly under her and tossed and turned to block her godfather's moves. The next morning she called her father and tearfully related the incident. Her father refused to believe her; he accused Desiray of making up the incident to get attention. Luckily, her mother realized that she was telling the truth and finally understood why Desiray had been so depressed the past year. Feeling that Desiray was probably not Streate's only victim and that he must be stopped, Desiray and her mother went to the police.

They soon found that securing a conviction against Richard Streate as not going to be easy. Attempting to build a case against him, the Simi Valley sheriff's investigators had Desiray make a recorded telephone call to Streate bringing up the molestation. During the forty-five-minute conversation, Streate carefully denied Desiray's allegations. There seemed to be no way to catch the abuser. But less than a year later, another young girl came forward to accuse Richard Streate of repeatedly molesting her over a three-year period. Faced with two similar complaints against him, Streate confessed his guilt.

Desiray showed a great deal of courage in pursuing the case. Fewer than half of child sexual abuse cases ever reach court. Many young victims are intimidated by the sometimes harsh realities of the justice system; others simply do not wish to face the perpetrator again.

The detective working with Desiray explained what was involved, but the young girl was determined to continue. She even went a step further than court. In order to avoid the stigma associated with the crime, most sex-abuse victims to not reveal their identity. But Desiray let the media know who she was and why she was determined to see justice served. "I felt like I had to do that for the other children," she stated, " 'cause I know that there were tons just like me that are out there and weren't talking."[25]

"I never knew another child that had done it," Desiray's mother added. "She would change the world. She'd be the first child, the first girl in the nation that I knew of that would say, 'I was molested, and this is my name.' "[26]

Desiray wrote to Gloria Allred, a respected feminist attorney, asking her to take on her case and cause. Ms. Allred agreed, and once Desiray Bartak had her day in court Richard Streate was sentenced to three years in prison. But Desiray Bartak had not finished her trailblazing in the realm of children's rights. Desiray initiated a civil suit against Streate to compensate for the physical and emotional damage done to her. "I knew that you had to do something to get somewhere in life," she said in describing her motives for the civil suit, "and what I would like to see coming through this lawsuit is more kids coming forward about it. And I want them to know they can do this."[27]

To spread the word to children throughout America and encourage them to recognize their rights, Desiray Bartak and her mother founded Children Against Rape and Molestation (CARAM). Desiray also writes a newsletter that is widely distributed to victims'-rights groups and to police officers who deal with youthful victims. Many children who've been through experiences like Desiray's have written to her. Besides support, the advice she gives is direct and action-oriented: "If they have already been through the abuse, I tell them that I think they should file a police report and I think that if no one listens to them, they should keep on telling until someone will listen to them."[28]

Although many people applauded Desiray's choices as heroic, she paid a price for her actions. Some students at her school accused her of leading her godfather on. She was criticized, badgered, and even chased home. As a result of such incidents Desiray eventually had to leave school to study at home. Since her father refused to believe her, speaking out also harmed Desiray's relationship with him.

But despite these personal consequences, in January 1994 Desiray Bartak was awarded more than $2 million in damages. It's doubtful that Desiray will ever collect the sum, since Streate isn't wealthy. But many believe the legal and emotional strides she made for young people are worth more than money.

Deborah Weisman is another young woman who made a valuable contribution to children's rights. Deborah grew concerned about the issue of religion in the schools when she attended her older sister's 1986 graduation from a Rhode Island public junior high school. Deborah felt uncomfortable during the commencement ceremony as a Baptist minister led everyone present in prayer. "I have always felt that religion is important and has its place, but I don't think a public school is the place," she said.[29] Deborah's parents wrote to school authorities expressing their daughter's sentiments, but they never received a reply.

Several years later when Deborah was about to graduate from the eighth grade, her parents again contacted the school to raise this issue. The Weismans, who are Jewish, were told that now a rabbi as well as a minister would be present to say some words at the ceremony. It was clear that the school hadn't understood Deborah Weisman's objection. She wasn't upset because a minister rather than a rabbi had spoken, but because she didn't think prayer had a place in a public school.

The local school board did not agree with the Weisman family's assessment of the situation. Claiming that prayer had long been a graduation tradition, the board chose to disregard the objections and keep things as they had been. That left the young graduate with few alternatives, although the school board had told the Weismans that if they didn't like their decision, they could sue.

In response Deborah and her family contacted the Rhode Island chapter of the American Civil Liberties Union, or ACLU. When an ACLU lawyer won the resulting court case, the school board appealed the verdict. After the Weismans won for a second time, the school board appealed again. Finally the case was heard before the United States Supreme Court, which determined that prayer in public schools violates the First Amendment of the Constitution. However, the determination came nearly three years after Deborah Weisman's eighth-grade graduation.

It wasn't easy for the young teen and her family to take on the school system. Deborah described what it was like for them: "Throughout the years of waiting for a ruling we were harassed by hate mail and even death threats; and the media attention often bothered me. But I was encouraged by the support we received from friends and at no time did I regret having taken our case to court."[30] Deborah's success in making the school recognize her concerns was an important student victory, with ramifications for young people throughout America.

In all the cases described in this chapter, young people stood up for their rights when it wasn't easy to do so. Besides fighting for the principles they believe in, they've served as role models for countless other children and teens. Without intending to they became trailblazers for the rights of minors; they've shown that a young person's voice can have a potent impact.

5
Liberation or Protection?

Whereas most people agree that children need both physical and emotional nourishment to thrive, there are differing opinions as to the best way for them to secure it. "Child liberationists" feel that children should be legally entitled to the same rights and privileges as adults. They think that minors need to be respected rather than protected and patronized and believe phrases like "Childhood is golden" are merely outdated clichés. In making their case, they point to the fact that protective agencies chartered to assist children have frequently fallen short of the mark, in some cases even making decisions detrimental to young people they serve.

Child liberationists argue that while youths might not always wish to exercise all the rights enjoyed by adults, it's important for them to be able to do so. They feel that children should have the right to decide whether their home lives are satisfactory, and should, if they wish, be permitted to establish their own residences. If these young people are unable to support themselves, child liberationists want them to be eligible for welfare benefits just as adults are.

They also assert that children should have the right to work and believe that many youths who are bored and unmanageable in the classroom might be stimulated and better off in the workplace. Child liberationists think that work could give young people a glimpse of the future and make them feel like needed and important members of society.

They also suggest that since individual rights need legal backing, minors should be permitted to vote so that they can elect officials who support their interests.

Perhaps the child-liberationist viewpoint has been best summarized by psychologist Richard Farson, who thinks that "our world is not a good place for children . . . [because] every institution in our society discriminates against them. . . . Our society refuses to recognize their right to full humanity."[1]

But, Farson suggests, the status of children is ripe for change: "The civil rights movement and the various liberation efforts which it has ignited have alerted us to the many forms oppression takes in our society. As a result we are now seeing the children as we have not seen them before—powerless, dominated, ignored and invisible."[2] Farson along with others who share his sentiments would ideally like to see the following rights accorded to all young people:

CHILD'S BILL OF RIGHTS

1. The Right to Self-Determination. Children should have the right to decide the matters that affect them most directly.

2. The Right to Alternative Home Environments. Self-determining children should be able to choose from a variety of arrangements: residences operated by children, child-exchange programs, twenty four hour child care centers, and various kinds of school and employment opportunities.

3. The Right to Responsive Design. Society must accommodate itself to children's size and to their need for safe space. [The reasoning here is that children would not need to be so rigidly controlled if their surrounding physical environment were less dangerous.]

4. The Right to Information. A child must have the right to all information ordinarily available to adults—including, and perhaps especially, information that makes adults uncomfortable.

5. The Right to Educate Oneself. Children should be free to design their own education, choosing from among many options the kinds of learning experiences they want, including the option not to attend any kind of school.

6. The Right to Freedom from Physical Punishment. Children should live free of the threat from those who are larger and more powerful than they.

7. The Right to Sexual Freedom. Children should have the right to conduct their sexual lives with no more restriction than adults.

8. The Right to Economic Power. Children should have the right to work, to acquire and manage money, to receive equal pay for equal work, to choose trade apprenticeship as an alternative to school, to gain promotion to leadership positions, to own property, to develop a credit record, to enter into binding contracts, to engage in enterprise to obtain guaranteed support apart from the family, to achieve financial independence.

9. The Right to Political Power. Children should have the vote and be included in the decision making process.

10. The Right to Justice. Children must have the guarantee of a fair trial with due process of law, an advocate to protect their rights against their parents as well as the system, and a uniform standard of detention [the same standards of punishment in all fifty states].[3]

Still another child liberationist, author John Holt, underscores these sentiments: "I have come to feel that the fact of being a child, of being wholly subservient and dependent, of being seen by older people as a mixture of expense, nuisance, slave and super pet, does most young people more harm than good."[4]

Others concerned for child welfare have a different perspective on improving the lives of young people. "Child protectionists" favor enhancing benefits and services for youths within such existing social constellations as the traditional family, the public school system, and juvenile court. Child protectionists believe that, rather than confer adult status on children, adults must remain aware of the needs of children and act as a strong voice in their defense. This can take the form of lobbying elected officials for reform concerning national child and family policy as well as urging professionals working with children to make the child's overall welfare their primary concern.

In assessing the children's rights movement, psychologist Judith S. Mearing identified the following six areas in which it has had a positive impact on the ethics and behavior of professionals working with children and/or their families:

1. The children's rights movement has challenged us to examine the origins of our beliefs concerning a child's best interests.

2. The children's rights movement has revealed the complexity of protecting children in our routine procedures.

3. The children's rights movement has helped to expose the autocratic use of the individual professional's power and judgment.

4. The children's rights movement has stimulated professionals to reconsider ways of responding to parents.

5. The children's rights movement has heightened professional concerns with gaps in services, discrepancies between the way children should be served and the way in which they are actually served, and the policy implications.

6. The children's rights movement has underlined the necessity for individual professionals to go beyond traditional ethical guidelines and to take personal risks to serve children's best interests.[5]

In order to enhance the well-being of young people in the United States, a number of protectionist child-advocacy groups have arisen. Among the most active of these is the Children's Defense Fund (CDF). Child advocate and attorney Marian Wright Edelman founded the organization and has described its fundamental purpose as "an attempt to create a viable, long-range institution to bring about reforms for children."[6] In addition to assisting children in other areas, the CDF has worked for political and legal change in the juvenile justice system, child-development programs, and services for youths with special needs.

The thrust to improve children's and teenagers' lives has been international in scope as well. The United Nations has long worked on behalf of children around the globe. The fifty-four articles of the UN Convention on the Rights of the Child have been hailed as a Bill of Rights for young people. The convention was adopted by the United Nations on November 20, 1989, and put into action on September 2, 1990, after being ratified by a sufficient number of nations. The convention is further-reaching than previous similar efforts; it addresses such pressing issues as the special needs of refugee children, the plight of children in armed conflicts, and the fate of children in trouble with the law.[7]

Regardless of the good intentions of child advocates, the fight for children's rights remains an uphill battle. In the difficult economic climate of the 1990s, many Americans have been more interested in lowering taxes and reducing the national debt than in pouring funds into social programs to assist young people. The children of many other nations, too, have received only a fraction of what's needed. Considering this attitude and the continuing high incidence of child abuse and neglect, it's clear that children's-rights activists face a serious challenge ahead.

Appendix I

Know Your Rights

While some youths have waged court battles and media campaigns to establish their rights, others have accepted less-than-desirable situations because they didn't know their rights. Ascertaining the rights of minors can be somewhat complex, because legislation often varies in different states. However, the questions and answers below provide an idea of what young Americans can expect as well as what's expected of them in some important areas:

Question: Are minors entitled to financial support from their parents?
Answer: Parents are obligated to provide such basics as food, clothing, shelter, and medical care. However, specific amounts to be spent raising a child are not specified by law. So adequate clothing can be everything from hand-me-downs from relatives and family friends to fashionable, expensive designer clothes and running shoes.

If parents divorce, their obligation to their offspring remains. But a stepparent who has not legally adopted his or her spouse's child is not bound by law to support that young person.

Question: Do minors have a right to keep money they've earned?
Answer: Surprisingly, the answer to this question is no. Although parents are legally obligated to support their children, they are, in turn, technically entitled to the youth's earnings. The reasoning behind these laws dates back to colonial America, when farm families often had children to help with the work. Although a parent can collect an offspring's wages from his employer, many parents allow their children to keep all or a substantial portion of what they earn.

Some states have passed special legislation to protect the earnings of minors who make a great deal of money, such as child actors and models, or others in high-paying professions. In these cases a special contract between a minor and an employer can be drawn up so that the wages either go directly to the youth or are placed in a trust account until he or she reaches adulthood. However, the minor's parents or legal guardian must give consent before such an agreement can be put into effect.

Question: Can minors sign an apartment lease or have a will?
Answer: No.

Question: Do young people have the right to sue?
Answer: Yes. As demonstrated by the nationally reported suits launched by Gregory Kingsley, Kimberly Mays, and Desiray Bartak, children have the same right to sue as any adult.

Question: Can young people be paid less than minimum wage because of their age?
Answer: In industries in which minimum wage laws apply, employers are obligated to pay minors that rate or more. Some classes of employment not covered by minimum wage laws include household work, agriculture, certain service industries, and numerous state and federal government jobs.

Question: Can a minor inherit money, valuable jewelry, or real estate?
Answer: Yes. Children can inherit money, property, and articles of value. If the person from whom they inherit specifies that the funds or valuables be placed in trust until the young person reaches maturity, the minor cannot take control of the assets until the specified time.

Question: Can a pregnant young woman still attend regular classes and engage in extracurricular activities at her school?
Answer: Pregnant young women have the same right to education as any other students. They cannot be legally barred from class or from school activities such as glee clubs, science fairs, or the school newspaper.

Question: Can a minor have an abortion without her parent's knowledge?
Answer: Technically, minors have the same right to abortion as any woman, but some states have passed laws requiring young women (under eighteen) to either notify their parents or even secure their parents' consent. As an alternative, a young woman who lives in one of these states can appear before a judge to ask that the requirement be waived in her case.

Question: Can a public school student refuse to be strip-searched by a teacher or other school employee?
Answer: Strip searches of public school students are illegal in many states. In places where they aren't outlawed, strict guidelines must be followed in ordering and carrying out such measures. School officials must have a strong reason to suspect that the student being strip-searched is guilty of serious wrongdoing.

Question: Can school personnel search a student's locker?
Answer: Court rulings on this question vary from state to state. Many state courts have decided that since lockers are school property, they can be searched at any time. However, in other states, courts have ruled that a student's locker cannot be searched unless school authorities have good reason to believe it contains something illegal.

Question: Can a teacher strike a student?
Answer: In at least twenty-two states corporal punishment—hitting—in public schools is against the law. Other states still permit corporal punishment, but require that it not be "unreasonable and unnecessary" or "excessive."

Question: What rights does a minor have if stopped and questioned by the police upon leaving school?
Answer: According to the American Civil Liberties Union's 1993 pamphlet "Ask Sybil Liberty: Your Right to Due Process," if the police tell a minor that he or she is suspected of a crime and then go on to ask questions, the young person should immediately state that he or she wants a lawyer. The organization advises, "Never, never try to talk your way out of whatever it is. Always ask for an attorney, and don't give any information except your I.D. It's legal for a cop to frisk you if he or she has reason to believe you are concealing a weapon. If he or she asks to search you and/or your car, don't resist the search but make it clear that you're not consenting to it."

Question: What rights does someone under eighteen have if arrested?
Answer: In most states minors arrested for crimes are not dealt with in the adult criminal-justice system. Instead they are treated as "juveniles" and their cases are heard in a special court known as juvenile court. Minors charged, tried, and convicted of a crime are often put on probation, ordered to attend a special rehabilitation or education program, or sentenced to do time in a juvenile detention facility.

Question: Under what circumstances can a student be suspended from school?
Answer: States have varied laws regulating the grounds for which a student may be suspended. Suspension is considered a serious penalty, and educational authorities usually don't resort to it casually. Usually, a student is only suspended if he or she has committed an illegal or dangerous act at school or has been repeatedly disruptive.

Question: What recourse does a suspended student have?
Answer: Any student suspended from public school has a right to know the precise reason why. He or she has the right to challenge the suspension through a hearing before an impartial board, as well. Students suspended for a long period can be represented by an attorney at such hearings. The suspended student's attorney may call and question witnesses, and the accused youth also has the right to have a record of what's said at these proceedings.

Question: Does a student have the same right to a hearing if he disagrees with a teacher or other school authority over any disciplinary action?
Answer: The ruling in the 1975 U.S. Supreme Court case *Goss v. Lopez* guarantees students the right to a hearing in serious disciplinary actions such as suspension or expulsion. However, students are not entitled to a hearing for such disciplinary measures as being made to stay after school or having to write an essay on "why I should not talk to my friends during class."

Question: Does a gay or interracial couple have a right to attend a school prom even if the school has a policy prohibiting it?
Answer: All students, regardless of their race or sexual orientation, have the same rights and are entitled to equal privileges at school. At least one court case in which a gay student wished to have a male prom date was decided in the student's favor.

Question: What recourse does a student have who feels he's been given lower grades or overlooked for special honors because of his race or religion?
Answer: Discrimination of that sort by teachers or other school personnel violates both state and federal laws. If speaking up about what's happening doesn't end the discrimination, the student may take legal action.

Question: Does a student who's tested positive for the human immunodeficiency virus (HIV), which causes AIDS, have the right to attend public school even if the school board prefers that a tutor come to his or her home instead?

Answer: It has been medically shown that AIDS cannot be transmitted through casual contact, so HIV-positive students pose no threat to their classmates or teachers. The right of such students to attend public school is protected by the Americans with Disabilities Act (ADA). This legislation also guarantees the HIV-positive young person or adult the right to use public swimming pools, restaurants, stores, museums, and other public places.

Question: Does a young person who recently came to the United States with his or her family have the right to go to public school even if the family members aren't citizens?

Answer: Anyone living in the United States, regardless of nationality or legal status, is entitled to the same rights as a citizen. This includes a free public education as well as access to corresponding opportunities such as school clubs, athletic teams, and other school-sponsored programs.

Question: Can a student wear a button, jewelry, T-shirt, or cap bearing a printed message or insignia?

Answer: Any student has the right to wear an article of clothing or an accessory reflecting his or her feelings or beliefs, as long as the message does not interrupt the education process. The right to do so was underscored in the 1969 U.S. Supreme Court decision in *Tinker v. Des Moines Independent Community School.* In that case the court affirmed the right of students protesting the Vietnam War to wear black armbands to class: "It can hardly be argued that either students or teachers shed their constitutional rights to freedom of speech . . . at the schoolhouse gates."

Question: Can a public school student wear whatever clothes and hairstyle he or she wishes?

Answer: The answer to this question depends on where the student lives. In some areas courts have ruled that a student's clothes and hairstyle are his or her own concern unless they somehow present a safety hazard to the student or to others. In other parts of the country, courts have determined that schools can impose both hairstyle and dress codes on their students. At times school authorities have argued that dress codes are necessary to curtail gang violence, since some colors and clothing styles indicate gang affiliation.

Question: Must a student say the Pledge of Allegiance at school assemblies and other functions?

Answer: A student cannot be forced to recite the pledge if he doesn't wish to. Some students who are atheists refuse to say the pledge because it mentions God. Other young people have refused to say the Pledge of Allegiance as a silent protest against a government action or policy they strongly disagree with.

Question: If a student writes an article for a school newspaper on a controversial topic (such as dispensing condoms in school) that the administration doesn't feel belongs in the publication, does the student still have the right to have it printed?
Answer: Usually the school officials will win out in these situations. In the 1988 case *Hazelwood School District v. Kuhimeier,* the U.S. Supreme Court held that schools have a right to curtail student expression in official school publications as well as in school activities such as drama productions.

Students are still free to express their views, but they cannot use school-sponsored channels to do so. Therefore, such young people would need to print and distribute their own pamphlets or leaflets. As long as these materials are not inflammatory or disruptive, the students are within their rights.

Question: What is emancipation and how can a young person achieve that status?
Answer: "Emancipation" is the term used to describe the process by which a minor is legally granted adult status in society. This means that his or her parents are no longer obligated to provide support and are not responsible for the young person's actions. In turn, the minor cannot be controlled by his or her parents and is not required to give them any portion of his earnings. An emancipated minor assumes all the rights and responsibilities of an adult.

Minors who wish to become emancipated will usually have to appear in court. In evaluating such requests, judges consider the minors' age, their ability to support and care for themselves, whether or not they live at home, whether they pay their own debts, what their spending habits are, and additional related factors.

There are other conditions under which minors may become fully or at least partially emancipated as well. Some youths live independently as emancipated minors through an informal arrangement between their parents and themselves. Under these circumstances the young person frequently establishes his or her own residences and lives as an adult. A minor who marries or joins the armed forces is automatically emancipated since such a lifestyle change generally constitutes a transition into adulthood.

Question: Can an emancipated minor still attend public school?

Answer: The majority of states permit young people to continue their public school education whether or not they live at home. Yet in some areas school boards have attempted to bar emancipated students on the grounds that they must be able to contact an adult responsible for the student if medical or disciplinary problems occur. Some school officials have also stressed that the untraditional lifestyles of minors living without parents could have a negative influence on the other students. However, these arguments tend not to hold up in court.

Appendix II

Organizations Concerned with the Welfare of Children

Americans for International Aid
435 Wavetree
Roswell, GA 30075-2928

Association of Administrators of the Interstate Compact on
   the Placement of Children
c/o American Public Welfare Association
810 1st St. NE, Suite 500
Washington, DC 20005

Association of Child Advocates
P.O. Box 280
Bloomfield, NY 14469

Child Abuse Institute of Research
P.O. Box 1217
Cincinnati, OH 45201

Child Abuse Listening and Mediation
P.O. Box 90754
Santa Barbara, CA 93190-0754

Child Find of America
P.O. Box 277
New Paltz, NY 12561

Child Welfare Institute
1365 Peachtree St. NE, Suite 700
Atlanta, GA 30309

Child Welfare League of America
440 1st St. NW, Suite 310
Washington, DC 20001

Children, Inc.
P.O. Box 5381
1000 Westover Rd.
Richmond, VA 23220

Children of the Americas
P.O. Box 140165
Dallas, TX 75214-0165

Children's Aid International
6720 Melrose Ave.
P.O. Box 480155
Los Angeles, CA 90048-1155

Children's Committee
P.O. Box 16133
Fresno, CA 93755

Children's Defense Fund
122 C St. NW
Washington, DC 20001

Children's Foundation
725 15th St. NW, Suite 505
Washington, DC 20005

Children's Rights of America
655 Ulmerton Rd., Suite 4A
Largo, FL 34641

Children's Rights Group
543 Howard
San Francisco, CA 94105

C.H.U.C.K.
P.O. Box 188
Sayville, NY 11782

Clearinghouse on Child Abuse and Neglect Information
P.O. Box 1182
Washington, DC 20013

Committee for Children
172 20th Ave.
Seattle, WA 98122

Defense for Children International—United States of America
210 Forsyth St.
New York, NY 10002

Find the Children
11811 W. Olympic Blvd.
Los Angeles, CA 90064

Grandparents'/Children's Rights
5728 Bayonne Ave.
Haslett, MI 48840

Grandparents Raising Grandchildren
P.O. Box 104
Colleyville, TX 76034

Institute for the Community as Extended Family
232 E. Gish Rd.
San Jose, CA 95112

International Child Resource Institute
1810 Hopkins
Berkeley, CA 94707

International Society for Prevention of Child
  Abuse and Neglect
1205 Oneida St.
Denver, CO 80220

National Child Support Advocacy Coalition
P.O. Box 420
Hendersonville, TN 37077-0420

National Council for Children's Rights
220 I St. NE
Washington, DC 20002

Organization for the Enforcement of Child Support
119 Nicodemus Rd.
Reistertown, MO 21136

Orphan Foundation of America
1500 Massachusetts Ave. NW, Suite 448
P.O. Box 14261
Washington, DC 20044-4261

Parents Sharing Custody
420 S. Beverly Dr., Suite 100
Beverly Hills, CA 90212-4410

Paul Andrew Dawkins Children's Project
P.O. Box 11008
Fayetteville, NC 28303

World Children's Day Foundation
4401-A Connecticut Ave. SW, Suite 287
Washington, DC 20008

Youth Ambassadors International
P.O. Box 5273
Bellingham, WA 98227

Source Notes

1. IN WHOSE BEST INTEREST?

1. Jon D. Hull, "The Ties That Traumatize," *Time*, April 12, 1993, p. 48.
2. Ratu Kamlani, "In Whose Best Interest?" *Time*, July 19, 1993, p. 49.
3. Ibid., p. 47.
4. Ibid., p. 46.
5. Hull, op. cit., p. 48.
6. "Tot Faces Transfer to Biological Parents," *The Star Ledger*, Newark, N.J., July 29, 1993, p. 3.
7. Ibid.
8. Ibid.
9. Ibid.
10. Michelle Ingrassia and Karen Springer, "She's Not Baby Jessica Anymore," *Newsweek*, March 21, 1994, p. 66.
11. Kamlani, op. cit., p. 49.

2. A SHAMEFUL HISTORY CONTINUES

1. Beatrice Gross and Ronald Gross, eds., *The Children's Rights Movement: Overcoming the Oppression of Young People* (New York: Doubleday, 1977), p. 28.
2. Ibid., p. 30.
3. Robert Brenner, *Children and Youth in America: A Documentary History, 1600–1865* (Cambridge, Mass.: Harvard University Press, 1970). Vol. 1, p. 38.
4. Ibid., p. 273.
5. Gross and Gross, op. cit., p. 115.
6. Walter I. Trattner, *Crusade for Children: A History of the National Child Labor Committee and Child Labor Reform in America* (Chicago: Quadrangle Books, 1970), p. 72.

7. Ibid., p. 27.
8. Joseph M. Hawes, *Children in Urban Society: Juvenile Delinquency in the Nineteenth Century* (New York: Oxford University Press, 1971), p. 91.
9. Elizabeth H. Pleck, *Domestic Tyranny: The Making of Social Policy Against Family Violence from Colonial Times to the Present* (New York: Oxford University Press, 1987), pp. 69–75.
10. Joseph M. Hawes, *The Children's Rights Movement: A History of Advocacy and Protection* (Boston: Twayne, 1991), p. 49.
11. Ron Chepesick, "Peonage for Peach Pickers," *The Progressive*, December 1992, p. 22.
12. Ibid.

3. THE RIGHT TO PROTECTION FROM ABUSE AND NEGLECT: ONE STEP FORWARD, TWO STEPS BACK

1. Peter Stevens and Marian Elde, "The First Chapter of Children's Rights," *American Heritage*, July/August 1990, p. 84.
2. Ibid., p. 87.
3. Ibid., p. 88.
4. Ibid.
5. Ibid., p. 89.
6. Ibid., p. 90.
7. Ibid.
8. Jean Carey Bond, *A Force for Change; Children's Rights Project of the ACLU* (New York: American Civil Liberties Union, 1993), p. 1.
9. Ratu Kamlani, "In Whose Best Interest?" *Time*, July 19, 1993, p. 48.
10. Karen Dorros and Patricia Dorsey, "Whose Rights Are We Protecting Anyway?" *Children Today*, May/June 1989, p. 8.
11. Bond, op. cit., p. 1.
12. Ibid., p. 2.
13. Ibid., p. 3.
14. Ibid., p. 11.
15. Ibid., p. 5.
16. Ibid., p. 13.
17. Ibid., p. 6.
18. Ellen Wulfhorst and Barbara Goldberg, "The Steinberg File," *New York*, April 17, 1989, p. 44.
19. George Hockett, "A Tale Of Abuse," *Newsweek*, December 12, 1988, p. 53.
20. Ibid.
21. Ibid.

22. Philip Shenon, "A Flogging Sentence Brings a Cry of Pain in the U.S.," *The New York Times*, March 16, 1994, p. 1.
23. Ibid.
24. "Yank Teen is Caned Amid U.S. Protests," *The Star Ledger*, Newark, N.J., May 6, 1994, p. 1.

4. STANDING UP FOR THEIR RIGHTS

1. Pat Weingert and Eloise Salholz, "Irreconcilable Differences," *Newsweek*, September 21, 1992, p. 85.
2. Ibid.
3. Ibid.
4. Ibid.
5. Ibid., p. 86.
6. Ibid.
7. "A Child Asserts His Legal Rights," *Time*, October 5, 1992, p. 22.
8. *Oprah*, "Divorcing Your Parents," February 9, 1993. Transcript, p. 4.
9. "Swapped Teen Granted Wish to Keep Dad Who Raised Her," *The Star Ledger*, Newark, N.J., August 19, 1993, p. 12.
10. Jean Seligman, "Stirring Up Muddy Waters," *Newsweek*, August 30, 1993, p. 58.
11. "Swapped Teen," p. 12.
12. Ibid.
13. Ibid.
14. "Looking for Shelter," *Newsweek*, March 14, 1994, p. 66.
15. *Oprah*, op. cit., p. 2.
16. Ibid., p. 4.
17. Ibid., p. 13.
18. Ibid., p. 21.
19. Ibid., p. 23.
20. *ABC News 20/20*, January 28, 1994. Transcript, p. 2.
21. Ibid.
22. Ibid.
23. Ibid.
24. Ibid., p. 3.
25. Ibid., p. 4.
26. Ibid.
27. Ibid.
28. Ibid., p. 5.
29. "Ask Sybil Liberty; Your Right to Religious Freedom." No au-

thor given (New York: American Civil Liberties Union, 1993).
Unpaged pamphlet.

30. Ibid.

5. *LIBERATION OR PROTECTION?*

1. Joseph M. Hawes, *The Children's Rights Movement: A History of Advocacy and Protection* (Boston: Twayne Publishers, 1991), p. 115.
2. Ibid.
3. Beatrice Gross and Ronald Gross, *The Children's Rights Movement: Overcoming the Oppression of Young People* (New York: Doubleday, 1977), pp. 327–28.
4. John Holt, *Escape from Childhood* (New York: Ballantine Books, 1984), pp. 1–2.
5. Judith S. Mearing, "Ethical Implications of the Children's Rights Movement for Professionals," *Harvard Educational Review*, February 1974, pp. 53–54.
6. "An Interview with Marian Wright Edelman," *Harvard Educational Review*, February 1974, pp. 53–54.
7. "The Convention on the Rights of the Child," *UNESCO Courier*, October 1991, p. 39.

For Further Reading

Cummings, Rhoda, and Gary Fisher. *The Survival Guide for Teen-agers With LD*. Minneapolis: Free Spirit, 1993.

Davenport, Terilyn. *Starting Out: Step-by-Step Guide for Teens Suc-ceeding in the '90s*. Cupertino, Cal.: Step-by-Step Publications, 1994.

Dryfoos, Joy G. *Full Service Schools: A Revolution in Health and Social Services for Children, Youth, and Families*. San Francisco: Jossey-Bass, 1994.

Dunnahoo, Terry. *How to Survive High School: A Student's Guide*. New York: Franklin Watts, 1993.

Garrity, Carla B., and Michael A. Baris. *Caught in the Middle: Pro-tecting the Children of High-Conflict Divorce*. Lexington, Mass.: Lexington Books, 1994.

Gay, Kathleen. *Getting Your Message Across*. New York: New Discov-ery Books, 1993.

Johnson, Daniel. *The Consumer's Guide to Understanding and Using the Law*. Cincinnati: Betterway, 1994.

Kronenwetter, Michael. *Under 18: Knowing Your Rights*. Hillside, N.J.: Enslow Publishers, 1993.

Landau, Elaine. *The Right to Die*. New York: Franklin Watts, 1993.

Lifton, Betty Jean. *Journey of the Adopted Self: A Quest for Whole-ness*. New York: Basic Books, 1994.

Lindsay, Jeanne Warren. *Teen Dads: Rights, Responsibilities, and Joys*. Buena Park, Cal.: Morning Glory Press, 1993.

McKelvey, Carole A., and Stevens, JoEllen. *Adoption Crisis: The Truth Behind Adoption and Foster Care*. Golden, Col.: Fulcrum, 1994.

Nava, Michael, and Robert Dawidoff. *Created Equal: Why Gay Rights Matter to America*. New York: St. Martin's Press, 1994.

Quinn, Patricia O. *ADD and the College Student: A Guide for High School and College Students with Attention Deficit Disorder*. New York: Brunnel/Mazel, 1994.

Index

....